A Chilling History
of Crime and Punishment

Somerset

A Chilling History
of Crime and Punishment

Roger Evans

COUNTRYSIDE BOOKS
NEWBURY BERKSHIRE

First published 2009
© Roger Evans 2009

COUNTRYSIDE BOOKS
3 Catherine Road
Newbury, Berkshire

To view our complete range of books,
please visit us at
www.countrysidebooks.co.uk

ISBN 978 1 84674 175 3

Cover illustration
courtesy of
Paul Townsend,
www.gertlushonline.co.uk

Designed by Peter Davies, Nautilus Design

Produced through MRM Associates Ltd., Reading
Typeset by Mac Style, Beverley, E. Yorkshire
Printed by Information Press, Oxford

Contents

MAP OF THE OLD COUNTY OF SOMERSET

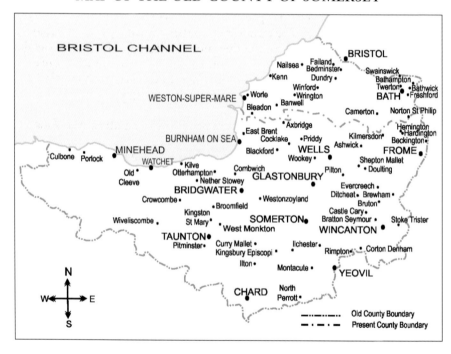

BRISTOL CHANNEL

BRISTOL

Nailsea • Failand • Bedminster •
• Kenn Dundry • Swainswick •
Winford • Bathampton
• Wrington Twerton • • Bathwick
Banwell BATH • Freshford
• Worle
WESTON-SUPER-MARE
Bleadon •
Camerton • Norton St Philip •

• Axbridge
East Brent • Hemington •
• Hardington
Cocklake • Kilmersdon • Beckington •
BURNHAM ON SEA • • Priddy Ashwick •
Blackford • WELLS FROME
Wookey •

Culbone • Porlock • MINEHEAD Shepton Mallet •
WATCHET • Kilve • Doulting
Old Otterhampton • Combwich Pilton •
Cleeve • Nether Stowey GLASTONBURY
Evercreech •
BRIDGWATER • Ditcheat • Brewham •
Crowcombe • • Westonzoyland Bruton •
• Broomfield Castle Cary •
Kingston SOMERTON • Bratton Seymour • Stoke Trister •
Wiveliscombe • St Mary • WINCANTON
West Monkton
TAUNTON •
Pitminster • Curry Mallet • Ilchester • Corton Denham
Kingsbury Episcopi • Rimpton •
Ilton • Montacute • YEOVIL •

N

W ← → E CHARD • North Old County Boundary
S Perrott • Present County Boundary

INTRODUCTION

———— ✠ ————

Somerset's rich history is packed with curious crimes and peculiar punishments waiting to be discovered. In the following pages, I endeavour to reveal some of the most fascinating along with the most tragic. Delving into curious crimes can reveal a list of felonies that would create a challenging round of 'true or false' quiz questions. Try the following and decide for yourself which are plausible enough to be true:

- Castle Cary's lock-up was once used to imprison children who failed to attend Sunday church service.
- Somerset's transvestite Mary Hamilton was so convincing as a man that she married 14 different wives before being discovered and subsequently publicly whipped.
- Clipping bits of metal from the edge of coins would earn you the death penalty.
- After the Monmouth Rebellion, hundreds of Somerset men were sold into slavery to work in the West Indian sugar plantations.
- Effigies of unfaithful husbands and wives were burned on bonfires as a public humiliation.
- The Magna Carta and the Domesday Book were stored in Shepton Mallet prison during the Second World War.
- Hundreds of Somerset men and women were transported to Australia on the convict ships for crimes as petty as stealing a handkerchief.
- American GIs were executed in Shepton Mallet prison, some by firing squad in which one member of the squad fired a blank – but no one knew who had the blank.
- A man who killed his wife would be hanged for murder. But a woman who killed her husband would be burned at the stake for committing petty treason.
- An Otterhampton vicar was once found guilty of smuggling.
- Jane Austen's socialite aunt was held prisoner at Ilchester gaol – but was allowed to live with the gaoler's family.
- Public executions became 'Hanging Days', like local bank holidays with Somerset crowds of 20,000 attending the events.

- Henry lll had the Magna Carta amended to make it a capital offence to kill or harm fairies. There were never any prosecutions for this offence in Somerset despite which no fairies appear to have survived.

Incredibly, they are all true and help to demonstrate just how much there is to discover in looking at local aspects of crime and punishment. Starting with the unusual crimes and horrific retribution of the medieval period, we explore the variety of punishments inflicted, including the official, the unofficial and the more entertaining ones imposed by local communities. The days of witchcraft are explored and Somerset witchcraft trials uncovered.

Highway robbery, smuggling, forgery and rebellion are all exposed, along with the penalties. We even take a look at life inside the Somerset gaols, Ilchester with its contrasting treatment for rich and poor, Wilton prison in Taunton with its front door executions and Shepton Mallet with its human tread-wheel. It all adds up to create a rich tapestry of intriguing stories and insights into Somerset's criminal past.

Roger Evans

1

How Times Have Changed

Medieval justice

Today we have no death penalty in Britain, nor do we have corporal punishment in schools. But such punishments existed until surprisingly recently, both in my lifetime. In terms of humane justice, we have travelled a long way in a relatively short space of time. Punishments that would appear abhorrent today were the norm in my childhood. In similar fashion, punishments deemed abhorrent in my childhood, when execution by hanging still existed, were quite acceptable in medieval times when the heads of executed victims were placed on spikes and left on town bridges as a message to would-be miscreants. Most Somerset towns and villages had their own local stocks, pillories and whipping posts, and every part of the county has born witness to public executions attended by tens of thousands of willing spectators.

Off with their heads

An early example of heads on spikes comes from Ilchester and Bridgwater in 1381. Unrest existed between Bridgwater's two principal churches, St Mary's and St John's. St Mary's was the town's first church but it was the relatively new St John's that took all the tithes and even appointed the vicar of St Mary's. Nicolas Frompton, a priest, and Thomas Engilby, a yeoman, raised a mob, acting on behalf of St Mary's. They raided the premises of St John's, took its leader for ransom and burnt various deeds as well as two properties, beheading Walter Baron, the owner of one of them. Then they made for Ilchester gaol where they removed Hugh Lavenham, who had been keeper of the gaol, had him beheaded and took his head on a spear back to Bridgwater. There it was displayed on the town bridge alongside that of Walter Baron. Despite the horrific nature of the crimes, no one was ever punished.

Another case of execution by beheading comes from Bridgwater Castle. Within its walls were the various apparatuses of punishment: stocks, pillories and ducking stool. One example of the ultimate punishment was the execution of Humphrey Stafford, the Earl of Devon, who had displeased Edward IV by failing to support the Earl of Pembrokeshire in an assault on the Yorkshire rebel known as Robin of Redesdale in 1469. The king was furious and declared that the Sheriffs of Somerset were to 'make diligent search for Humphrey Stafford, Earl of Devon, and execute him without delay'. He was captured at Brent Marsh, near Brent Knoll, and taken to Bridgwater Castle where he was beheaded on 17th August in that year.

Was this the only execution within the castle? Almost certainly not. When the foundations were being dug for sheltered accommodation for the elderly, which was built along the line of the castle moat in Chandos Street, a number of skeletons were found. The strange thing was that the heads were separate from the bodies! The remains were gathered together and re-interred in Wembdon churchyard.

Even the Abbot of Glastonbury wasn't exempt from losing his head. At the time that Henry Vlll dissolved the monasteries, Richard Whiting, the 80-year-old Abbot of Glastonbury, resisted the changes. He paid the ultimate price for defying the king and was hanged on Glastonbury Tor. After his execution, his body was quartered. His white-haired head was displayed on the gates of Glastonbury Abbey whilst the quarters were distributed to be put prominently on view at Bath, Wells, Ilchester and Bridgwater, where the grisly relic could be seen at the East Gate.

Mutilation

Before prisons were introduced in the 12th century, mutilation was used as a form of punishment and to indicate someone as a criminal. One of the villain's ears would be cut off for a first offence. A second offence would see the victim wave goodbye to the other ear after which, having run out of ears, the letter F would be branded on the forehead to indicate a felon. Further offences would result in the eyes being removed. Very few crimes were committed after that!

Medieval courts

Bridgwater also provides us with a useful insight into the system of courts and law enforcement. The burgesses of the town were that privileged band of people who had their own businesses and were allowed to hold their own court once a month on a Monday to deal with minor crimes – trespass, fraud, debt and environmental issues such as ditch clearance, the removal of offal, short measure, trading too close to someone selling the same items and regrating. This latter offence was committed when an item was bought and then sold at a higher price on the same day. Punishments included imprisonment, the pillory and the tumbrel or cucking-stool, all of which are dealt with later.

During the 14th century there were three systems of courts within the town. First, there was the borough court, which appointed two each of reeves, bailiffs, ale-tasters, bread weighers, a single janitor to attend the town gates and a group of wardens who kept an eye on the dozen or so streets in the town. They could impose fines for offences, and if the miscreant was unable to pay in cash, the court could demand possession of goods to the value of the fine, anything from a brass pot to a horse. Beyond fines came the tumbrel or cucking-stool, or worse still the pillory.

The second court was the Piepowder court, which survived from 1378 right through to the 18th century. The Piepowder court derived its name from the French for 'dusty foot', a reference to people on the move. It provided justice for merchants and travellers from outside the borough when attending the town's fairs and markets.

The third court was the Durneday court, which appears to be unique to Bridgwater. Its purpose was to ensure that the citizens or burgesses paid their tolls and rents. Durneday was the day on which the payment for the lease of a burgage (a parcel of land held in tenure for an annual rental) became due, normally sometime in January or February. Failure to pay up resulted in the court ordering the door of the miscreant's dwelling to be sealed until such time as the payment was settled. 'Durn' is the old Somerset word for the frame of a door. In 1468 there was a new charter for the borough and it appears that the three courts merged into one.

Borough archives from the early 1400s give an interesting insight into the way law and order was applied. Although the borough had two constables, and two bailiffs to collect fines, the maintenance of peace and good order was the responsibility of each individual living within the borough. Each townsman was expected to take his turn at maintaining vigilance in the town. One archived document shows a list of 279 names. Fines ranging from 1d to 4d (overwhelmingly the latter) had been imposed on those who failed to keep their watch. 'Vigilant' had been indicated against 55, showing that they had fulfilled their duty. Thus it tended to be the wealthy who paid to avoid such duty and the poor who were obliged to fulfil it.

County assizes

By the 17th century a system of travelling judges had been adopted whereby they would travel around the region holding their assizes for a set number of days. In Somerset these courts were held at Taunton, Bridgwater and Wells, and other towns according to the need. It was a system whereby a jury of good men and true were used to determine the outcome from the evidence produced. However, they didn't always come up with the result that the judge wanted.

In 1667 a Somerset jury found a man not guilty in a murder trial. Chief Justice Kelynge did not agree and told them that they had produced the wrong result and were to change their verdict. He threatened to have them thrown into prison with a hefty fine if they didn't do so. However, a report on this case refers to them getting away with it because they were deemed to be 'gentlemen of repute in the county'. It had not been an idle threat to imprison them. Elsewhere a jury were locked up for two days without food, drink, heat or light until they conceded to give the verdict requested by Kelynge. They refused, were fined 40 marks each, locked up again and remained there until another judge intervened and had them released. The mark was an old unit of currency used in England and Scotland, equivalent to thirteen shillings and eight pence, being two-thirds of a pound.

Another problem with these circuit judges was that their stay in any one town was limited, perhaps to five days at the most. If a jury was taking longer than normal to reach a verdict, the judge would be faced with the problem that the following day he was due to be elsewhere in another county. The jury had the choice of travelling with him to his next venue until they produced a verdict, or face a fine and possible imprisonment.

Attitudes to capital punishment

Although beheadings, burnings and other forms of execution were all practised from the 5th century onwards, hangings were the commonest form of despatch. Over the centuries attitudes to crimes have altered and the death penalty was once applied to a wide range of crimes, some seemingly very petty by today's standards. In 1713 the death penalty was introduced for theft of goods valued over £2. In 1723 poaching and damage to forests were added to the list and, in the next few years, the list of 30 capital crimes grew to an astounding 150 possible offences. By 1810 this had expanded to 222 possible felonies but in practice it was only applied to about 20 of these, with sentences almost predictably being reduced to transportation for the other offences.

In the early medieval period, there existed a loophole by which the death penalty could be avoided. The ecclesiastical courts were more lenient and any member of the clergy accused of a crime could claim 'benefit of clergy', which meant they would be tried by an ecclesiastical court rather than the general court. This way they avoided the death penalty but had first to prove that they were of the clergy, which only required that they could read a verse of Psalm 51. Some form of punishment was still required and in such cases transportation to America was quite common. Since 'benefit of clergy' could only be claimed once, a solution was to brand the thumbs of the individual concerned to indicate that their 'Get out of jail free' card had already been used.

An alternative way to escape the noose was to seek sanctuary at an approved church, such as the cathedral at Wells or Stogursey church where a sanctuary ring still exists. Once sanctuary was granted, the person concerned could move freely within a mile of the cathedral or church for the next 40 days. Once that time expired, then they had to walk barefoot carrying a cross to reach the coast, from where they had to leave the country. If no ship was ready to sail, then each day they had to walk into the sea at least up to the knees to indicate their intention to leave the country once a ship became available. Failure to do so would invoke the death penalty previously avoided.

In 1834 hanging in chains was abolished and by 1861 the list of capital offences had reduced to just four: murder, arson in a naval dockyard, high treason and piracy. All of these are covered in detail in the forthcoming chapters. The death penalty was provisionally removed in 1965, and effectively ceased at that time. But it should be remembered that it was as recently as 1998 that the Criminal Justice Bill finally removed the death penalty officially from our justice system.

2
CUCKING, DUCKING AND SKIMMINGTON RIDING

---- ✳ ----

Medieval days, and right through to the 18th century, provided a plethora of different forms of crime and punishment. Today we may joke about hen-pecked husbands, and cartoons poke fun at the battle-axe wife with her timid, cowering partner, but in medieval times it was a crime to be bullied in such a way. To make things worse, it was not the wife who was considered to be at fault but the husband for failing to keep her under control. Once married, she became his property and his responsibility. A wife who constantly found fault or nagged incessantly was considered to be a scold – and in this case it was she who was punished. A wife committing adultery was also a crime – and the husband could be punished as a cuckold, a man who had lost control of his wife. It may be from the word 'cuckold' that the cucking stool is derived, which was one of the forms of punishment used in such cases. It was applied to husbands for wife beating and to either party where a wife had committed adultery or excessive complaining, due to the husband's loss of control of his wife. Others punishments included the ducking stool, the tumbrel, stocks, pillories and whipping posts, all of which we explore here.

Public confessions
In cases of minor offences, the medieval solutions revolved around public humiliation and many of these methods lingered well into the 19th century. The simplest punishment, and probably used for the least serious offences, was public confession. In communities where the church had strong control, the culprit could be required to stay behind after mass and recite, in front of the congregation, the crimes committed. In market towns this was often carried out at the market cross. In either case it was important that there was maximum public exposure. In 1338 John de Middleton, who was the rector of Bleadon, sat in his church investigating a charge of improper conduct by Alice Manschupe from Blackford and Cristina Coker from Cocklake. Both women confessed and so were sentenced to walk barefoot around Banwell church, confessing their sins aloud as they did so, the sentence being carried out immediately.

Skimmington riding, bonfires and tumbrels

An alternative to public confessions was the informally organised skimmington riding. It was arranged by collaboration between offended neighbours and other members of a community, who took the law into their own hands. As the punishment was generally accepted as 'no more than they deserved', the authorities were happy to condone and even encourage such practice. It was applied to husbands for wife-beating, to adulterous wives and to either party if the wife complained excessively and her husband failed to control her.

Skimmington riding came in various forms depending on local custom. Generally speaking it was a noisy procession in which an errant husband or his wife were seated back-to-front astride a donkey, a pole or on the back of a cart, and then paraded through the village. The procession would be led by a band of 'rough musicians' who, in the cases of sexual misdeeds, would also carry cattle horns as an indication of the nature of the crime. Sometimes the couples would be partly spared the ordeal, perhaps by refusing to come out of their homes. In such cases, the villagers would dress up as the offending couple or use effigies. Thomas Hardy in his *Mayor of Casterbridge* describes such a scene thus:

> *The numerous lights round the two effigies threw them up into lurid distinctness; it was impossible to mistake the pair for other than the intended victims. 'Come in, come in,' implored Elizabeth, 'and let me shut the window!' 'She's me – she's me – even to the parasol – my green parasol!' cried Lucetta with a wild laugh as she stepped in. She stood motionless for one second – then fell heavily to the floor. Almost at the instant of her fall the rude music of the skimmington ceased. The roars of sarcastic laughter went off in ripples, and the trampling died out like the rustle of a spent wind.*

Skimmington riding shown on a wall plaque in Montacute.

Some Somerset villages still offer evidence of these events in their place-names, such as Skimmerton Lane at Wembdon on the outskirts of Bridgwater. At Curry Mallet, there was an ancient Skimmington Well where the 'Old Witch' would stand and dispense her cures, although knowledge of its location has long since been lost.

In Bridgwater, where the Guy Fawkes carnival is such a strong tradition, another form of public humilation was the burning of effigies on the bonfires, which began as far back as 1606. It may seem a tasteless comparison but I well remember the news broadcasts in the wake of the September 11th attack on the Twin Towers in New York. Television took us into the towns and villages of Afghanistan and Pakistan where effigies of George W. Bush were put to the torch by excited, exuberant crowds of fanatics. In their own way, they reflected those 17th-century celebrations much closer to home when the nation was divided on religious grounds and the failure of the Gunpowder Plot was celebrated with bonfires and the burning of effigies. The bonfire was used as a way for groups to publicly express their anger with individuals who it was felt had let down the community.

In 1860 an effigy was produced of a worker from the railway carriage works in Bridgwater. It appears this fellow had brought about the dismissal of a number of his colleagues, who took their revenge by parading his effigy, labelled 'A traitor to his shop mates', through the streets before committing him to the flames of the town's Cornhill bonfire. In 1867, in similar fashion, a farmer titled as 'The King of Dunwear', having rendered himself obnoxious to his neighbours, was given the same treatment in this 19th-century equivalent of 'naming and shaming'. In 1872 the Cornhill bonfire was host to the effigy of someone called the Yard Spy, presumably a reference to a tell-tale brickyard worker; the Salmon Parade bonfire was host to Brother B and Sister S, a widower and seaman's wife accused of an extra marital relationship; and the Barclay Street and Albert Street fires each consumed an effigy of alcoholic and unfaithful wives, one with a gin bottle suspended around her neck declaring its part in the unseemly behaviour of the miscreant. Even as late as 1906 an effigy of the minister of the Baptist Church was committed to the flames. He had unsuccessfully attempted to stop the pubs opening late on carnival night!

As a variant to skimmington riding and effigies on bonfires, the tumbrel offered another informal punishment executed by the local community. The tumbrel, a simple two-wheeled, hand-pushed cart, was most commonly associated with being the transport used to take a victim to the site of an execution. In Somerset, the tumbrel was used as a cart to carry stones for roadworks or more commonly for dung, this latter use adding to the humiliation. The victim would be transported thus around the community to be taunted and jeered. Now and again, when spirits were high, it would end with the tumbrel being run into the village pond.

Cucking stools

The cucking stool was a type of chair used as a punishment, partly as a minor form of torture but more commonly as a means of public humiliation, most commonly for scolding or nagging. Hence it was almost exclusively used to punish the ladies, the men being put in the stocks. In both cases, the passing public could hurl whatever abuse or offensive objects that took their fancy. As far back as the days of the Saxons it was used as a 'stool of repentance' to which a woman would be tied, her head and feet being bare. She was either left at her front door or carried aloft through the streets to the jeers of the crowds.

The cucking stool could occasionally be used for men, typically for brewers making weak beer or bakers producing underweight loaves. Where married couples were concerned, they could be tied to back-to-back chairs.

Although this punishment dates back to the Domesday Book in which it receives a number of mentions, the most popular period was the 17th century. 'The Cucking of a Scold', a ballad from the early 17th century, gives an insight into the use of the cucking stool:

> *Then was the scold herself,*
> *In a wheelbarrow brought,*
> *Stripped naked to the smock,*
> *As in that case she ought:*
> *Neats* tongues about her neck*
> *Were hung in open show;*
> *And thus unto the cucking stool*
> *This famous scold did go.*

The records for Banwell church in 1568 make reference to 'Paid John Payne for the Kooken stool, 17 shillings'. In Bruton in 1688, the constable was paid for the removal of the stocks from the river at Patwell Street, and then paid to replace them the following year with a new cucking stool and for mending the pillory.

Ducking stools

Ducking stools and cucking stools were very similar – the difference being, as the name suggests, that the ducking stool involved immersion in water, the local river or pond. Since the ducking stool would be taking rougher treatment, its structure had to be more robust. It was a strongly-built item, usually of oak, and was fixed to the end of a long wooden beam mounted on

---

*'Neats' is Old English for cattle and suggests that the cows' tongues were hung around her neck, indicating that it was her tongue that had caused offence.

a pivot to permit a seesaw action of lowering and raising the culprit. The victim, having been put in the chair, would be secured by an iron band around her waist. This both ensured that she did not fall out during immersion and also helped to prevent the chair from floating. Its use in Somerset crept in during the early 17th century. In rare cases, the ducking stool was mounted on wheels and simply pushed into the water, having been paraded through the streets, but this was perhaps more accurately a tumbrel rather than ducking stool. Imagine the scene – excited villagers enjoying the thrills and spills as the tumbrel was pushed haphazardly towards the depths of the river, laughter and frivolity all around. As they approached the banks of the river, the two handles used to push the cart were released and the cart careered down the bank into the cold river water.

The use of the ducking stool was a formal affair, not a spontaneous punishment as seen with skimmington riding. The magistrate would dictate the number of immersions based on the seriousness of what we would today view as petty offences. Occasionally the magistrate might oversubscribe and the lady concerned would die from drowning. In the early days of its use, it was also the preferred method for testing for witches and this is dealt with in more detail later.

Stocks and pillories

Medieval market places were dirty, smelly places. Anyone who has been to a fish market in the Far East can imagine the stench of a medieval market where scraps of fish and meat, decaying vegetables and other less pleasant deposits from the animals simply never got cleared away other than when the weather lent a hand. It was in such market places that the stocks were positioned, thus giving the benefit of maximum exposure for the villain and an ample supply of unpleasant matter to hurl at the unfortunate detainee. The stocks were a familiar sight and were basically a low-level leg clamp with the culprit sitting on the ground. There the unfortunate person would spend the required number of hours or days before release.

Records from as early as 1227 indicate the use of stocks and by 1405 legislation existed requiring every village to have its own stocks, in the absence of which the village would be downgraded to a hamlet. They had special importance after the Black Death in 1349. With so many deaths, the nation's workforce was dramatically depleted and it was critical that everyone should do a full day's work. Failure to do so would result in a visit to the stocks and possible facial branding.

One incident resulting in the use of the stocks took place at Lopen Fair, an annual event where there was plenty to eat and drink, and with entertainment such as bear-baiting, wrestling and cudgelling, a competition in which men attempt to club each other into a state of unconsciousness. One year a young student was proving to be a little too boisterous and so Sir

Amyas Poulett, the High Sheriff of Somerset, had the student locked in the stocks for disorderly conduct. The bright young lad was Thomas Wolsey who at the time was employed by the Earl of Dorset to educate his sons. That young lad was to become the Archbishop of York, Cardinal of Rome and Chancellor of England. Having achieved such high status, he remembered his adversary down in Somerset, the man who had him locked in the stocks, and had Sir Amyas placed under virtual house arrest for more than six years.

The pillory was a similar 'man-trap' where three holes in a horizontal line were positioned so that the head and the two wrists either side could be pinioned whilst the culprit was in the standing position. The pillory was therefore normally fitted to the top of a post to get the right height, unlike the low-level stocks. Also pillories could be positioned at crossroads as well as in market places and the entrapped individual would often have a sign hanging around his neck indicating the nature of his crime.

The pillory was introduced in Anglo-Saxon times, originally for slander, cheating with dice and for begging using someone else's child! It soon became the accepted treatment for cheating tradesmen. After 1637 it was also the accepted form of punishment for those who published anti-government material. Even Daniel Defoe was once pilloried for libel against the government but so popular were his views that flowers were thrown and he received a warm ovation from onlookers. The pillory was a form of both humiliation and torture with the villain being denied any food or drink, but worse tortures were also permitted.

William Prynne, who was born in Upper Swainswick near Bath in 1600, was one victim of the pillory for activities as a pamphleteer. Educated at Bath grammar school and then Oxford University, he studied law and became a fervent Puritan. He criticised actresses as 'notorious whores' when, unfortunately, Queen Henrietta Maria was appearing in a play! In 1637, he was brought before the court, found guilty of sedition and sentenced. In addition to a £5,000 fine and imprisonment for life, he was condemned to have his ears 'cropped'. From within the Tower of London, he continued to write articles critical of the clergy. These were smuggled out and published. Another court case ensued and he was sentenced to stand in the pillory and have the remainder of his ears removed, his nose slit and his cheeks to be branded with 'SL' for seditious libeller. Such was the way that justice was dished out in those days.

Although Prynne had his nose slit, more common was the slitting of the tongue whilst in the stocks, and frequently nailing of the ears. As early as the time of Queen Elizabeth l, there is evidence of such treatment. A statute introduced during her reign to reduce repetitive cases of forgery declared that everyone convicted of that crime should pay to the injured party double the value of the property, then be put in the pillory and have his ears nailed to it and have his nose slit before being seared with a red hot iron, subsequently

Bridgwater's old stocks now reside in Wembdon churchyard.

being imprisoned for life. Then, just to ensure justice was fulfilled, he should forfeit his goods and chattels to the Crown, and his lands and tenements. With such barbaric practices perhaps it was just as well that the pillory was abolished in 1837.

Still in use in the 18th century, Bridgwater's stocks and pillory, having spent 40 years outside of the Town Hall, were re-sited at the Cornhill. Those same stocks still survive today in Wembdon churchyard.

Stocks for the vicar

Stocks and pillories were common throughout Somerset. The church records for Banwell refer to the cost of mending the pillory in 1689 and to the cost of a new pillory built in the shambles area in 1716, still in regular use in 1738.

The Reverend John Skinner, whose diaries from around 1800 tell us so much about the north Somerset mining village of Camerton, recorded how unpopular he was and how he hated fulfilling his role in such a community. Aged 28 and with a background in law, which he had studied in London, he was totally unsuited to the life of a Somerset village. He recorded how he was 'heartily sick of the flock over which I am nominated' and how on one occasion he booted out the choir who apparently hadn't been sober since the day before. Is it any wonder he was treated discourteously? In 1822, his diary continued with:

I am tied hand and feet and placed in a pillory to be pelted at by Methodists, Catholics and Colliers; and moreover a combination of worthless farmers and an overbearing woman with an unprincipled steward to contend with.

Whilst the colliers of Camerton may have pelted their local vicar, it was other north Somerset miners who in 1732 went to the rescue of a Bristol-based Poor Laws guardian who had been found guilty of a 'filthy act'. In such cases, stoning was often linked with the pillory and could result in fatal wounds. The unpopular and very worried guardian paid for a hundred north Somerset miners to protect him from the crowd and he also wore a miner's helmet as protection. His flouting of the spirit of the law was soon to cause a riot and he had to be released before completing his alloted time at the pillory.

'I am tied hand and feet and placed in a pillory to be pelted at by Methodists, Catholics and Colliers ...': the Rev John Skinner of Camerton.

Whipping posts

Whipping posts were exactly as they sound, they were posts to which offenders, stripped to the waist, were tied in order to be flogged. This applied equally to women as it did to men and in such cases the order for the whipping would finish with the words 'till her body be bloody'.

In the village of Wraxhall, both the stocks and whipping post stood across the road from the village smithy where the Stumps Fair was held. In Compton Martin a whipping post was installed in 1770 alongside the pond and was used for cases of larceny, vagrancy and even for not turning up for church service. At Tintinhull, the still-existing stocks and whipping post were situated on the Green. At West Monkton the whipping post can be seen in the grounds of St Augustine's church. At Wrington the stocks and whipping post were repaired in 1747 and an early painting of Broad Street provides evidence of the position of the stocks outside the grounds of the Old Rectory, where a present day bakery can be found. Nailsea likewise can boast a former whipping post and stocks with repairs being recorded in 1700.

West Monkton churchyard holds the village stocks and whipping post. Notice the different sizes of wrist locks to cater for both children and adult offenders.

3

WITCHCRAFT

———————— ❈ ————————

Belief in witches was once so widespread in England that around 400 people were put to death for alleged witchcraft. Most of them were harmless old women living alone, persecuted by the superstitious and executed by the unjust. In medieval times, immersion in water was used as a 'foolproof' way of identifying the guilt or innocence of a witch. Whilst ducking stools, on the end of a long pole, were the original method, this was phased out in favour of the simpler method of tying the left toe to right thumb, and right toe to left thumb, before hurling the alleged witch into the water. Those who survived were condemned as witches on the assumption that they had been rescued by the Devil.

The last judicial murder of a witch took place in 1716, but as late as 1730, in Frome, an aged crone suspected of being a witch was forced to undergo the ordeal by water, watched by 200 taunting, cheering spectators. Half-drowned during the process, she was finally dragged from the millpond and dumped in a stable, where she died about an hour later. But before that event, there were centuries of witchcraft cases being tried across Somerset.

16th-century beginnings

It seems that when the witches weren't airborne, they were thick on the ground in Somerset. Perhaps the earliest recorded Somerset case of a witchcraft trial comes from Castle Cary in 1530 when Christian Shirston fell foul of her neighbours. Her situation was typical of so many at that time. Imagine in some bygone century, a woman visits a neighbour to ask for some food. The neighbour refuses and the woman walks away empty handed muttering, 'Well ****** you.' It's not a curse as such but, if something goes wrong very soon after, it will be viewed as a curse and hence the woman must have been a witch.

So it was for Christian Shirston. She was a poor woman who would go from door to door asking for bread, cheese, yeast, milk or ale. One September day she had twice been refused when asking for milk and ale. The following day, Joan Vicars' cow produced no milk and Henry Russe was unable to convert his milk into cheese 'until well after Michaelmas'. Isabel Turner, the ale brewer, found that her twelve gallons of ale suddenly and uncontrollably boiled away. There were undoubtedly natural explanations for these occurrences but it was sufficient to provoke a witchcraft trial.

Joan Tyrry was another Somerset witch trial victim. She was no more than a healer. Now my own grandmother knew numerous natural cures for various ailments from warts to morning sickness and my mother would read the tea leaves for our neighbours. Had they been around in the 16th century, they would have been classed as witches, the same as Joan Tyrry who claimed that she healed both man and beast by the power of God. Innocent enough but it was probably her claim that the fairies had taught her those skills that brought about her downfall.

In the final quarter of the 16th century, one per cent of all deaths were recorded as having been caused by 'blasting', or bewitchment, and it was during those years that we can find evidence that it was not just women who were tried as witches. In 1580 Henry Fize of West Pennard, Henry Harrison and Thomas Wadham all went to trial accused of witchcraft, specifically conjuration, which is the summoning up of demons or other evil spirits to cause harm to others or their property.

The 17th Century

If the 16th century had been difficult for both witches and innocents, the 17th century was to be intensely worse, a terrifying period through which to live and an era when 'witch hunt' was to enter our vocabulary as indicative of a reign of terror. Until such times, no one could really understand why those with the power to heal should be treated with anything other than respect. By the end of the 17th century, those with the knowledge passed down by generations of healers were too afraid to let their expertise be known. It was also the period when the name of Matthew Hopkins became famous as the Witchfinder General in East Anglia. In Somerset, we had our own witch finder, the magistrate Robert Hunt, who appears to have been only too ready to accept the flimsiest of evidence in order to convict.

Once again, it was not just the ladies who suffered. In 1626 Edmund Bull and Joan Greedie both went to the gallows under grave suspicion of being sorcerers. The flimsy evidence against them was accepted unchallenged. It was in August 1626, at their joint trial in Taunton, that the court was told how Edward Dynham suffered from fits. The pins and needles that he felt in his arms and hands, to us a perfectly natural occurrence, were described as 'sometimes they thrust pins and needles through his hands and nostrils of which he is insensible neither dost there any blood appear'. Suffice it to say that what would appear to be pins and needles and epileptic seizures were misunderstood and they were both sent to the gallows. With the exception of the investigation of two major covens near Wincanton in 1664, the only other recorded case of a Somerset male witch was in the case of a husband and wife, John and Agnes Knipp, also accused of conjuration at the Taunton Assizes.

Jane Brooks – the witch trial of 1658

One of Somerset's most interesting witchcraft trials came in Shepton Mallet in 1658. It was the well-documented trial of Jane Brooks who was accused of bewitching a 12-year-old boy, Richard Jones, by offering him an apple. He claimed that one morning in November 1657 she came to his home, where he happened to be on his own, and offered him an apple. The lad cooked the apple, ate it, and immediately fell violently ill. His father decided that the sickness was caused by Jane's evil powers and she was brought before two magistrates, Mr Carey and Mr Robert Hunt (our local witch finder) at Castle Cary on 8th December. As soon as the boy began his testimony, Jane stared fixedly at him, at which he lost the ability to speak. He remained dumb until she was taken from the room. Since no other evidence was offered, she was set free. But the witch hunt had begun and soon more serious accusations were laid against her, and she was imprisoned to await trial.

At the Chard Assizes in March 1658 she was tried for witchcraft by Sir John Glyn. Several witnesses claimed that Richard Jones was often to be heard making strange noises like the croaking of a toad, an animal generally associated with the black arts, repeating the name 'Jane Brooks' over and over. One woman insisted that she had seen the boy rise up from the ground in front of her eyes, ascending higher and higher so that he was lifted over the garden wall and swept along for about 300 yards, eventually crashing to earth at the front door of a Mr Jordan, where he lay as if dead for some time. When he recovered his senses, he told the woman that Jane Brooks had taken him up by the arms and flown with him through the air. Another witness swore that Richard had been found 'strangely hanging above the ground with his hands flat against the sides of a great beam in the top of the room and all his body two or three feet from the ground, and hath so remained a quarter of an hour at a time'. Nine other people agreed that they had seen the phenomenon.

Such damning evidence being impossible to disprove, Jane Brooks was found guilty of witchcraft and hanged on 26th March 1658. It's a pity that she wasn't given the same opportunity afforded to a lady in Wellington who was accused of numerous evil deeds. This lady demonstrated her innocence by reciting the Lord's Prayer word perfect at her trial – and was acquitted.

Julian Cox, Taunton Assizes 1663

Julian Cox was a beggar woman who would go from door to door seeking food and drink. She was a nuisance to her neighbours and an ideal target for a witchcraft accusation. The evidence against her proved that she was a 'witch in general' and that she had caused harm to a maid through the use of sorcery. In the case of the maid, it would appear to be another example of misunderstood epileptic seizures. Julian Cox was to take the blame for the action she had allegedly taken against the maid 'whereby her body languished and was impaired by reason of the strange fits upon account of the said witchcraft'. This turned out to be just one of a catalogue of incredible accusations.

A huntsman stated how on a day's outing with his pack of hounds, he had flushed a hare and the hounds had given chase. The hare headed for cover and slipped under a bush with the hounds close on its tail. The huntsman was right behind them, determined not to let them destroy the quarry, but when he got there, the hare was nowhere to be found. In its place was Julian Cox in a breathless heap, unable to utter a word. The hounds stopped their chase and stood over her, sniffing her as if she still held the scent of the hare. The poor huntsman was so terrified that he headed straight for home, fearing the worst that the witch may inflict on him.

Another witness stated how his cattle had been driven insane to the extent that they were ramming the trees with their heads. The advice given was to cut off and burn the ears of the cattle involved, effectively burning the witch's powers. This he did and no sooner were the ears on the fire, than Julian Cox turned up and removed them, from which point his cattle reverted to normal behaviour, albeit without their ears! A woman testified that Julian Cox had flown into her bedroom, in her full and normal form, so there could be no case of mistaken identity. A pipe-smoker complained that the witch had set an enormous toad to bother him as he sat to smoke his pipe. He took the offending creature home, cut it into pieces but it pieced itself back together again.

Then came the evidence apparently given by Julian Cox herself, but it was so self-condemning and damning that I can only believe that it was extracted under severe torture. She claimed that one evening, about a mile from her home, she met three people flying on broomsticks, two of them she knew to be a witch and a wizard, hanged many years before, and in all probability these were Edmund Bull and Joan Greedie who had been hanged at Taunton. The third person was unknown to her but offered to help her effect revenge against people who had wronged her, as long as she pricked her finger and gave her name in blood. But she was resolute and refused to co-operate. Perhaps she told this story to indicate her innocence but to no avail. Judge Archer announced the guilty verdict and condemned her to death. She was hanged four days later.

The Wincanton covens

The year 1664 saw the two largest series of witchcraft trials in the county when two separate witches' covens were investigated. It would appear that there were at least two covens and speculatively, based on the usual number for a coven being nine, I would hazard a guess at the following membership for three possible covens, based on the way that the names appear together in various court cases and references. The Wincanton, Brewham and Stoke Trister groups would appear to be near neighbouring covens:

Brewham coven
Margaret Agar
Catherine Green
Christian Green
Alice Green
John Syms
Henry Walter
 (churchwarden)
Dinah Warberton
Dorothy Warberton
Mary Warberton

Wincanton coven
John Vining
Thomas Bolster
James Bush
Christopher Ellen
John Combes

Richard Dickes
Thomas Dunning
Richard Larmen
Rachel King

Stoke Trister witches
Elizabeth Style
Anne Bishop
Alice Duke
Mary Penny
Margaret Clarke

In the expedition of witchcraft trials, there was a minimal requirement to produce hard evidence. Hearsay was submissible as was the testimony of young children, no matter how young and fanciful their imaginations may have been. Hence, and despite the incredibly unreliable evidence, there were far more trials than genuine witches to be tried. The vast majority of trials can be dismissed as time-wasting mischief on the part of feuding neighbours. Of all the witchcraft trials held throughout Somerset's history, the Wincanton trials of 1664 are by far the most informative.

These trials involved a number of local women: Elizabeth Style, a lady of nearby Bayford, about a mile and a half from Stoke Trister; Margaret Agar, an itinerant who had settled in Brewham; and Alice Duke, Mary Penny and Anne Bishop, who were all accused of practising witchcraft with Elizabeth at Stoke Trister. They were accused of holding meetings of witches' covens. Elizabeth Style had been accused of using witchcraft to inflict injury on several local people, including bewitching a 13-year-old girl. It was claimed that she had a pact with the Devil and that he would appear as a man, a cat or dog and even as a fly.

At her trial, presided over by Robert Jones, the court heard how Elizabeth Style made waxen images to inflict harm on those that she cursed. Margaret Agar was accused of having cursed Joseph Talbot to death, an accusation that would attract the death penalty if proven. Talbot was the local overseer responsible for the distribution of funds to the poor. Margaret had gone to him to appeal for assistance to clothe her children and had been refused; instead he put her sons into 'apprenticeships' – these were not as we know them today, but were forced-labour regimes in workhouses. Talbot had also taken her daughter into service. It would be enough to make any mother curse the man responsible, which she did, stating that he would never keep his job but would be carried out from it by four men. The following day, he died!

Beyond doubt, all of those on trial were severely tortured. In their confessions, they described how they would anoint their foreheads and wrists with a green oil, using a feather to apply the liquid, and that would allow them to be carried in flight to their meetings. There, on the common near Trister Gate and likewise in Wincanton churchyard, they would meet with the Devil who would arrive as a man in black and provide them with food and money before they were swept back to their homes. Alice Duke confessed that they would meet the Devil in the shape of a great black toad, which would leap up onto her apron. She also confessed to bewitching to death the wife of a man called Swainton and to cursing his cattle.

For the duration of the trial, Robert Jones appointed three men, William Thick, William Read and Nicholas Lambert, to watch over Elizabeth Style. Nicolas Lambert left a well-documented account of his experience. In the early hours of the morning, an inch-long brilliantly-lit fly rose from her head and settled on the chimney before disappearing. Style then became a ghastly black as the fire itself changed colour. Her hair shook and out flew what the three men described as a Great Miller, a butterfly, which settled on the table momentarily before disappearing. Style claimed it was just a butterfly but later confessed that it was her 'familiar'. It was to be the first of a number of visitations in which the creature would take the form of a bird, a polecat or even a greyhound.

The women were all inevitably found guilty and sentenced to death. Elizabeth Style was perhaps the lucky one in that she was never taken to be executed. Instead she died in prison, almost certainly from the effects of torture.

Christian Green, who was 33, survived the trials. The parish records show her as dying in 1709. She confessed to Robert Hunt that Katherine Green, her mother-in-law, had explained to her how she could escape the abject poverty to which she had fallen by making a covenant with the Devil. She could meet him, dressed in black clothes, on Brewham Common. She later met him there and Margaret Agar and Mary Warberton were already with him. She also claimed that Margaret Agar visited her and said that she should go to Husseys Knap in Brewham Forest to meet the Devil there. It was probably this 'evidence' that allowed her to go free.

A poem collected by C. Somerville Watson around 1896, which has been passed down by oral tradition, relates in part the recollections of the people of Stoke Trister:

> *But scarce had the bell pealed its sad, mournful notes,*
> *When all the good people at Stoke with hoarse throats*
> *From yelling and screeching in numbers were flocking*
> *To the home of the witches. It was really shocking*
> *To hear the bad language they used when they said*
> *They would pull the three women right out of their beds,*
> *And burn their old cottage right over their heads*
> *In return for the cruelty done to the dead.*

Further witch trials took place, mostly at Taunton: Anne Slade 1670; Margaret Stevens 1672; John and Agnes Knipp 1674; Martha Rylens 1675; Anna Rawlins 1680; Anna Clarke and Elenora, Susannah and Marie Harris 1683; Honora Phippan 1686; Margaret Coombes, Elizabeth Farrier and Ann Moore 1690; and Margaret Waddam 1694.

Common sense creeps into the 18th century

By 1700 the persecution of witches had taken a long overdue calmer approach. Gone were the hysteria trials of the troubled 17th century. The year 1707 saw first the trial of Maria Stevens in Taunton and then three women who had been accused of witchcraft by Mary Hill, an 18-year-old girl from Beckington. They were imprisoned in Bruton where one died before coming to trial. Part of Mary's case against them was her vomiting of over 200 nails and pins and various brass pieces. Their trial was held in Taunton but Mary lacked credibility and the purge against witches was coming to an end. The two survivors were released.

In 1736 witchcraft finally ceased to be a capital offence. However, whilst the authorities now seemed to be taking a more realistic approach to accusations of witchcraft, the people at large still fervently believed in the power of sorcery. In Crowcombe in 1725 the church spire was struck by lightning and crashed on the worshippers as they sheltered in the church porch. Despite this being a natural phenomenon, the local belief was that it was the work of witches.

The 19th century

By the 19th century the judiciary no longer held witchcraft trials, but there was still clear evidence that country folk took it seriously. There was a case reported in the *Bridgwater Times* of 14th September 1854 in which witchcraft was used as a defence in a case of assault. Alan Lamb, who lived with his mother in North Street, Corton Denham, suffered from epileptic fits. He believed that he had been bewitched by 39-year-old spinster Mary Crees, a glove maker, who lived in Victoria Cottage with her 76-year-old mother Fanny and her sister Elizabeth.

The matter came to a head at the Corton Friendly Society Fair. Lamb was a strong young lad, in stark contrast to Mary. When having a seizure it would take six men to hold him down. At the fair, and with a few drinks inside him, he approached Mary and angrily accused her of cursing him with the seizures. He took her by the throat and hit her several times in the chest. She did her best to ignore him, saying she had no idea what he was talking about. Half an hour later, he was back, this time with a knife. Dragged away by his gang of friends, he shouted that he would be back and that if he couldn't kill her then, he would wait for the chance.

At his trial, a witness explained on his behalf that there was no intention to kill Mary, only to draw blood in the belief that this would cancel the curse and bring his fits to an end. Lamb explained to the magistrate that Mary Crees had 'overlooked' him, which in old dialect translates as having given him the evil eye, and drawing blood was the only way to break the spell.

When the magistrate explained that Mary had nothing to do with Lamb's fits, the young man's response was that whilst that may be the opinion of the magistrate, he knew better and the magistrate would have a different opinion if he too suffered from the curse. The message wasn't sinking in and so the chairman of the court helped to explain. He told Lamb that Mary couldn't possibly harm him and so he wasn't to touch her. He was delighted, believing that the court had just told Mary that she was not to touch him and on that basis promised to behave in future. He was bound over to keep the peace. Common sense was beginning to prevail.

21st-century witchcraft

Is witchcraft now a thing of the past? Well, it's no longer a crime and so even the most respectable of people are willing to give it a try. In January 2004 Frome Town Football Club were positioned mid-table in the local football league and had hit a losing streak at their Badger's Hill ground. They were scoring ten times as many goals in their away games as at home. Perhaps the home turf was cursed. Rather than just rely on the ability of the players, it was decided to bring in the services of a local white witch, Titania Hardie, to lift the curse by surrounding them with a huge amount of positive energy.

Then, in January 2008, the Reverend Chris Horseman resigned from his ministry at Yatton when he decided to take a training course to be a white witch. Thank goodness the world is now more understanding and increasingly tolerant.

4

UNFAIR FOR THE FAIRER SEX

It wasn't only for witchcraft that women were condemned. Between 1740 and 1845 across the nation there were some 2,000 women sentenced to death for charges ranging from murder to pick-pocketing. Of those, around three-quarters were mercifully reprieved on appeal, particularly where the crime was one against property, theft for example, but rarely where murder or treason was involved. In the majority of cases, those reprieved were transported, either to America (until the country declared independence) or Australia. However, if they returned before they were due back, they were considered to be 'at large', an offence that then guaranteed the death penalty if caught. If we ignore those who were reprieved, this still leaves us with around 500 who were executed. In Somerset, their crimes broke down roughly as follows:

50%   Murder in its various forms
        20% murder of a bastard child
        10% petty treason (murder of husband)
        20% other murders
35%   Robbery in its various forms, house-breaking, pick-pocketing etc
15%   Various other crimes such as arson, high treason (for coining) and forgery.

Some of these require explanation. Arson attracted the death penalty because it was considered to be putting life at risk. Forgery and coining potentially could undermine the country's financial systems, hence they were considered treasonous.

Murder of a bastard child
The murder of a bastard child was relatively common. There was a tremendous stigma to the birth of a child out of wedlock. The mothers were usually young girls, many of whom would have been in service, and they and their illegitimate children became the financial burden of the parish. People

were poor enough without that additional cost and hence such young women were often ostracised by the community and indeed there were times when conceiving a bastard child was considered an act of lunacy, which would land the girl in an asylum. Was it any wonder that young expectant girls would do all in their power to hide their secret, to conceal the pregnancy from the community and to 'lose' the child once born? It was as late as 1922 that the Infancy Act removed the death penalty for such a crime, part of the reason being that there had been many cases where a child had been still-born but the mother was still accused of murder, or where the child had died of natural causes soon after the birth.

However, becoming pregnant also provided a delay in the execution of the death penalty for women. Hence, once condemned, they would often plead 'their belly', claiming to be with child. In such cases, they would be regularly examined by medical staff who would sooner or later be able to confirm whether or not the condemned woman was telling the truth. If not, they were executed but if they were genuinely carrying a child, the execution would be delayed until after the birth. Some women would do anything to avoid execution, including getting themselves pregnant, either through the services of a warder or a visitor.

Petty treason and burning

Burning, as a penalty, was basically reserved for cases of witchcraft (by either sex), heresy and high or petty treason. The earliest record we have of burning at the stake in Britain dates back to 1222 when an Oxford church deacon adopted Judaism in order to marry a Jewish woman. It was an act of heresy. In the mid-16th century, there were over 270 burnings for heresy, mostly

A 17th-century burning by
the artist Jan Luyken.

simply for people choosing the Protestant faith. It was particularly favoured by those with Roman Catholic beliefs, who considered that burning denied the body the opportunity to pass into the next life. Although most people associate burning at the stake with witchcraft, the commonest punishment for that offence was actually hanging.

In Britain there were two favoured methods of burning. The first was to produce a large pile of faggots, bundles of sticks, piled up around the base of the stake, and the victim would then stand on top of the pile, chained in irons to the stake. The second method was for witches where the victim was first tied to the stake and then the faggots piled up around her. These effectively screened the witch from view by the spectators, thus hiding her suffering. In the early days of burnings, the victim would be burned alive. However, during the reign of Mary I, a concession was introduced whereby the lady for burning could have a pouch of gunpowder around her neck. Clearly when this exploded she would feel no further pain. Latterly, and within the law, the victim would be strangled or part strangled first, to reduce the suffering. This was done by passing a rope around the neck and through a hole in the stake. At the moment of the fire being lit, the executioner would tighten the rope to effect the strangulation. On occasions, the flames would flare up too rapidly to allow this to be safely completed and the executioner would be forced back by the intense heat. In Somerset most of the cases of burning were for women who had committed the crime of petty treason.

It may seem odd that such a high number of women were condemned to death for petty treason. This needs some explanation. If a man acted against the interest of the king or country, it was considered to be treason, high treason. This included counterfeiting money or 'coining', which was the act

Hurdles were used to drag victims to executions.

of trimming bits off genuine gold or silver coins in order to create enough metal to produce fake coins. Such crimes were considered to be high treason and, for such, men were hanged but women, committing exactly the same crime, were burnt at the stake. It may seem unfair that women should suffer a more prolonged agony than the men, but the reason is historical. For the very worst of crimes, the men were hung, drawn and quartered. This involved dismembering their bodies, which was deemed distasteful for a lady. Hence they were burned.

In the same way that all men were considered to be the subjects of the monarch, and acts against the monarch were high treason, a married woman was considered to belong to her husband, in a similar master-subject relationship. Hence an act against a husband was treason, petty treason. So when a wife murdered her husband – or a mistress her lover – she was not tried for murder, but for petty treason and the penalty was burning at the stake, not hanging. At least two Somerset women suffered death by burning. In the case of burnings, the guilty person was dragged to the place of execution on a hurdle, which we would recognise as a sledge made in the form of a fence panel of woven branches. And it was never a case of ladies first. If there were multiple hangings to be carried out on the same day, the men would be hanged first and then the women would be led past the hanging bodies on the way to their own execution. In 1790 the laws changed and burnings were replaced by hanging for both petty and high treason.

Those who suffered in Somerset

At least fourteen women were executed during this period in Somerset. In all probability there were others but their records no longer exist. Those discovered are as follows:

For murder:	Place of execution
1740 Elizabeth and Mary Branch*	Ilchester
Murder of their maid servant	
1754 Mary Ashford	Taunton
Murder – hanged with her husband	
1845 Sarah Freeman	Taunton
Murdered her brother Charles	

For murder of a bastard child:	Place of execution
1747 Susanna Way	Taunton
1772 Elizabeth Mansfield	Bridgwater
1781 Martha Wills or Willis	Bridgwater
1793 Joan Tattel of Monkton	Taunton

For petty treason or murder of husband:	Place of execution
1753 Susannah Bruford*	Wells
Burned at the stake	
1765 Mary Norwood*	Ilchester
Burned at the stake	
1836 Sofia Edney	Ilchester

For other crimes:	Place of execution
1753 Elizabeth Gammin	Not known
At large	
1754 Elizabeth Barnstable	Not known
Stealing from a dwelling house	
1761 Jean Blave	Ilchester
Burglary	
1787 Grace Bootle	Ilchester
Burglary	

* Those marked with an asterisk have their stories related below.

The suffering of these women was very similar in all cases, as they were hanged by the 'short rope' method. This was unlike the trap-door method, which was introduced much later and, in theory, broke the neck instantly, thus reducing the physical distress. With the short-drop method, the victim of the execution would have her arms pinioned to her body, then she would be placed on the back of a cart and taken to the place of execution, usually a pre-erected gibbet in a field or common open place for maximum viewing. She would be given the opportunity to express her penitence and perhaps utter a prayer before the halter was placed around her neck and a cap placed over her head. The cart would then be pulled forward and she would drop gently, often with a faint and stifled scream, suspended by her neck, in great agony, her hands flailing up and down, her elbows pinioned to her side. The time to die could be estimated at around half an hour. If it sounds barbaric, that's because in reality it was, with the newspapers frequently using expressions such as 'she died hard'.

Death by burning, from a 17th-century woodcut engraving.

Elizabeth and Mary Branch

One of Somerset's worst ever examples of cruelty to a young child provides the background to the story of Elizabeth Branch and her daughter Mary, who were to hang together for their crimes. Elizabeth is believed to have been born in Norton St Philip. She had the reputation, even as a child, of being an extreme bully. However, someone clearly found her attractive since she married a wealthy farmer by the name of Branch from the nearby village of Hemington. He was a complete contrast to Elizabeth, a caring master to his servants.

From the very start of the marriage, she badly mistreated the servants, beating them and, on occasions, making them sleep outside irrespective of the weather conditions. Her husband did his best to keep her excesses under control but she was too powerful a character to be moderated.

A child, Mary, was born to the couple and soon learned from her mother, being equally cruel and villainous in her temperament. The husband died, leaving the mother and daughter to manage the farm and its team of servants, who now feared the worst from this abusive pair. Indeed their suffering increased to the extent that those who survived only did so by escaping from Elizabeth's clutches.

By 1740 Mary was full-grown, a 24-year-old, and shared her mother's passion for cruelty. Their reputation had spread far and wide around the district and there was not a servant or labourer, with any sense, who would put a foot anywhere near their farm. With no workers left, they had to rely on the parish to provide them and they started taking orphans from the poor house. Jane Butterworth, aged just thirteen, was such an orphan and fell victim to the couple. She was a simple girl who found learning difficult and soon became the centre of their cruel attention.

Matters came to a head when Jane had been sent to buy some yeast. Perhaps she was enjoying the brief moment of relative freedom and lingered too long in the market place. On her return she was accused of having returned too late for the yeast to be of any use. Both mother and daughter beat her, one using a shoe and the other hitting her mercilessly with a broomstick until her back was raw and bleeding profusely. The mother and daughter then literally rubbed salt into her wounds. The poor girl must have died in absolute agony.

A milkmaid, Ann Somers, had witnessed the beginning of the punishment but had left to tend to the cows. Perhaps she walked away simply to avoid witnessing what was going on. Whatever the reason, on her return to the farmhouse, she saw Jane's body lying in a pool of blood. Elizabeth meanwhile was warming herself in front of the fire. One would expect any normal person to show some remorse at having committed such a heinous act, but not Elizabeth. Instead she ordered Ann Somers to sleep with the body overnight and they would sort things out in the morning. Perhaps then it began to sink in that they could be in serious trouble and so, with a change of plan, in the middle of the night Elizabeth and Mary dragged the body across the fields to find a place to bury it.

Understandably, Ann Somers felt vulnerable. Having witnessed the murder, she had to consider the possibility that she could be the next victim as the only other person who could provide the required evidence. In a state of panic, she made her escape and headed off to find the police and report the crime. The body was soon found and exhumed. The result of the subsequent autopsy was that the girl had clearly died from the most violent criminal action. The arrest of Elizabeth and Mary Branch followed shortly after.

Mary wept as her mother gave the full details, confessing their joint involvement in the crime. The result of the trial in March 1740 was predictable and both were found guilty of murder and sentenced to hang. Early in the morning on 3rd May, they were executed at Ilchester, in the Gallows Field, swinging by their necks for over an hour before being cut down.

Susannah Bruford

All executions at one time were held in public and this provided opportunities for eye-witness accounts to be recorded and, needless to say, the reporters from various papers would turn out in force. Such was the case with Susannah Bruford whose public execution drew what was described in the press as a 'prodigious Concourse of People'. Perhaps it was all the more attractive as a spectacle since it was a burning rather than a hanging.

The background to the case began with the marriage of 19-year-old Susannah to a farmer near Taunton in the March of 1753. She was several years younger than her husband and was soon tempted by the advances of an attorney's clerk. An affair began and the plot instigated to slowly poison her new husband. Within six months of their marriage, she had been found guilty of his murder and condemned. The execution took place at Cure Green, near Wells, on Monday, 3rd September 1753. The *Salisbury Journal* for 17th September recorded the details of her final moments as follows:

> ... *She was had out of the Star-Inn in Wells about Four o'Clock in the Afternoon, dress'd in Black, with a Black Hood over her Face, and drawn on a Sledge, with a Hurdle and Pitch Barrel thereon, to the Place of Execution; where a Clergyman attended, with whom she spent about Half an Hour very devoutly in Prayer: She was then had to the Stake, and put on a Stool, with the Halter about her Neck; where after standing a few Minutes, earnestly begging for Mercy, she dropt a black Handkerchief which she had in her Hand, as a Signal to the Executioner, who thereupon instantly strangled her with the Halter; and*

having fastened the Body to the Stake, by two Iron Hoops, to support it, the Faggots were placed round, with a Pitch Barrel in the Middle, and Fire set thereto, which burnt furiously near an Hour: In which Time the Body was almost consumed, and the small Remains were put in a Coffin, and carried away to be interred.

It was never recorded as to whether or not the attorney's clerk was there to witness the death of the woman whose fate was so closely linked to his actions.

Mary Norwood

Another lady burned at the stake was Mary Norwood from Axbridge. She had also murdered her husband by poisoning. It was May 1765 and Joseph Scadding was the gaoler at Ilchester where Mary was held pending her execution. At 3 o'clock in the afternoon, she was taken barefoot from her cell. Her arms and legs had been tarred and a tarred simple, straight dress covered her body. In like fashion, her head was covered in a tarred cap, the tar melting in the sun and running down her face. She was placed on a hurdle and dragged to the place of execution, the Gallows Field.

Placed precariously on a tar barrel, she sang hymns and prayed as the executioner placed the rope around her neck, which she then adjusted to her own satisfaction. The barrel was rolled away, leaving her dangling in mid-air until the twitching subsided, at which point she was secured to the stake with irons and the surrounding fire lit. Whilst many of the large crowd would have looked away at the final stages, Joseph Scadding was obliged to look on, responsible as he was for ensuring the job was properly done.

5

SLAVERY FOR
MONMOUTH'S REBELS

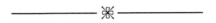

The whole of the 17th century had been troubled with religious conflict. Somerset was Protestant and when the Catholic James ll came to the throne, following the death of his brother, it was the Protestant James, Duke of Monmouth who was favoured by West Country folk, Monmouth being the son of the late king, albeit born outside of wedlock. So it was no wonder that when Monmouth decided in 1685 to take the throne by rebellion, it was to the West Country that he came and sought support.

The 1685 rebellion
The plan was that the Duke of Argyle would start a rebellion in the north, drawing the king's troops away, whilst Monmouth landed in Dorset and headed north to Somerset to start the rebellion there. Landing at Lyme Regis, he soon had 3,000 volunteers. Moving north to Chard and Taunton for a coronation, his army swelled to 7,000. Onwards to Bridgwater, to a civic reception and another coronation at the Cornhill. In the days that followed, he led his newly-born army around north Somerset with the odd skirmish against the king's troops. But there was a stark contrast between the two armies. The king's were battle-hardened, professional soldiers. Monmouth's men, in the main, were West Country yeomen and peasants, lacking military experience but fired up with religious fervour, fighting for the right to practise their religion as they saw fit.

Monmouth heard the news of Argyle's defeat in Scotland. No longer would the king's forces be divided. He needed to act fast. Lord Feversham with his Royalist troops had by now arrived and were camped at Westonzoyland, with 2,000 foot and 700 horse soldiers. The camp had the benefit of the Bussex Rhyne on two sides and a line of cannon on the other. It would be difficult to defeat other than by a surprise night attack.

The battle
At 11 o'clock on the evening of 5th July 1685, Monmouth led his troops out of Bridgwater and silently approached the enemy encampment. With just the

Bussex Rhyne to cross, a musket was accidentally fired and the alarm raised. The initial attack that followed was successful, but eventually repelled when the Royalists turned their guns on their attackers. From then on, the outcome was inevitable.

Artillery fire followed by cavalry charges resulted in hundreds lying dead on the fields of Sedgemoor. Monmouth escaped, only to be caught some days later, disguised as a woman, and he was later executed in the Tower of London. Back on the battlefield, the slaughter continued. Monmouth's rebels were mercilessly hunted down, and bodies were hung from trees along the Bridgwater to Glastonbury road. Five hundred rebels were locked up in Westonzoyland church; 22 were hanged on the way there, then five men died in the church and nineteen from that group were hanged the following day. The routing continued as troopers rode through the fields, tracking down hidden rebels. Many were shot for the sport, like hares being flushed out for the guns.

Retribution

The battle over, Feversham was recalled to London and was replaced by Colonel Percy Kirke. He had a special role to play. The king had ordered Judge Jeffreys to conduct the trials of the rebels, trials that were to become known as the Bloody Assizes. These, he was told, had to be wrapped up in days, rather than months. There was to be no opportunity for another rebellion to simmer beneath the surface. Kirke softened up the rebels to the extent that all pleaded guilty − even if they weren't. His technique was to invite the rebels to plead innocent or guilty. Those who pleaded innocent were immediately taken outside and hanged. It acted as a great incentive to the others to plead guilty.

During this period, Kirke lodged at Marycourt in Bridgwater, a building now called the Carnival Inn, in order that he could watch the hangings on the Cornhill in Bridgwater. One of those due for execution was Roger Hoar who, having been sentenced to death, was taken to the Cornhill but reprieved just in time when his family delivered and forfeited the deeds to his property, an almost guaranteed way to gain a pardon. Two years later he was Mayor of Bridgwater and now lies buried in St Mary's churchyard.

Into slavery

Hundreds were executed: hung, drawn and quartered. Over 2,000 were transported into slavery in the West Indies. Whilst this may sound an idyllic posting, it must be remembered that we are talking about the 17th century and those deported would have been crammed into the sweaty holds of small sailing ships for weeks on end, and those who survived that journey were then put to work as slaves in sweltering heat, receiving the same cruel treatment as the black slaves.

Deep in the Somerset countryside, well away from the unseemly trade in human beings, wealthy families built their grand homes using the profits from plantations that benefited from slavery. Henry Hobhouse, whose family were slave traders, acquired property in Castle Cary; Caleb Dickinson, owner of a Jamaican plantation, purchased King Weston House in Somerton; East Coker Court near Yeovil was home to the Helyar family, owners of sugar plantations in Jamaica; the Tudway family of Wells owned plantations in Antigua, rarely if ever visiting the islands where they would have witnessed the appalling conditions to which hundreds of their slaves were subjected. The wealth of these few families depended entirely on slavery. By 1685, at the time of the Monmouth Rebellion, slavery was in full swing.

In total, 612 Somerset men, Monmouth's rebels, were transported into slavery and sailed in eight ships to the West Indies. Many died during the voyage, others died on the quayside awaiting their auction. Within four years, the survivors were granted free pardons but most lacked the fare home. Those who returned told their families and communities of life as a slave. No wonder then that it was Bridgwater which was the first town, in 1785, to petition Parliament for the abolition of slavery.

6

HIGHWAY ROBBERY

———————— ※ ————————

The 18th century was the busiest time for highwaymen, who were as abundant in Somerset as elsewhere. Unlike smugglers (see Chapter 8), they had no popular support – it was the highwaymen who put fear into the otherwise enjoyable experience of travel. Smugglers, on the other hand, were seen as 'Robin Hoods', the kind people who helped the poor by evading high excise duty on imported goods. The executions of highwaymen were eagerly anticipated public spectacles, almost a tourist attraction. The case of William Hawkins demonstrates how these events were great crowd pullers, which of course was exactly what the authorities wanted. A notice in the *Sherborne Mercury* of 21st April 1741 called upon the officers of the Sheriff of Somerset to gather a week later at nine in the morning at Robert Fry's house in Chard in order to attend the execution of William Hawkins who was to be hanged in chains on Chard Common on that day. Quite clearly this not only acted as an instruction to the Sheriff's officers, but was also an invitation to the general public to witness the event. William Hawkins was just one of many.

Thomas Lympus, highwayman

Thomas Lympus began his working life as a messenger boy for the General Post Office. In that role he became familiar with the high value of so many of his deliveries. He opted for a change of career, preferring robbing to delivering the mail. In February 1738 he began his plundering by stopping the post-boy as he was delivering mail destined for Bristol and Bath. Having snatched sufficient promissory notes, he headed for the coast and escaped to France. An Act of Parliament had already granted a significant reward for evidence leading to arrest in such cases, despite which the Postmaster-General added a further £200 for any information. The hunt was on for Lympus, who was described on the wanted posters as a middle-sized man with a large riding coat and a white plush or velvet cape. With such an accurate description, information was soon received as to his French whereabouts. With the authorities close on his heels, he prudently adopted the Roman Catholic religion, which then allowed him to seek sanctuary in the church.

Thomas Lympus, highwayman. From the *Newgate Calendar*, 1738.

In time he became frustrated. He was unable to pass the stolen notes in France and made his return to England. No sooner was he back in the county than he re-offended, this time holding up the post-boy as he left Crewkerne destined for Sherborne. Lympus made the boy dismount and then bound him hand and foot before riding off with 24 bags of mail, including a large quantity of banknotes. Once again he fled, making for France, but the winds blew his ship back ashore and he took shelter at Dartmouth. Foolishly he tried to pass one of the stolen notes but by this time the alarm had been raised and the banknote was recognised. With a posse of seven men in hot pursuit, he was captured as he headed back towards Somerset and was taken to trial at Wells. There he was convicted of robbery and sentenced to death by hanging. Facing the inevitable, he confessed to all of his crimes and was taken to Dulcote Hill, less than a mile from the centre of Wells. There on 21st September 1739, professing Catholicism as his adopted religion, he met his maker.

John Poulter alias Baxter, highwayman

There appears to be no reason why John Poulter should have slipped into a life of crime, yet he was still to become one of Somerset's most prolific highwaymen. Born in Newmarket, he received adequate schooling and aged thirteen was given employment as a stable hand with the Duke of Somerset, a position he maintained for the next six years. With a perfect reference, he was recruited into the service of a Colonel Lumley for whom he frequently took racehorses to France, and perhaps it was here that he developed wanderlust. In the years that followed he travelled as a sailor to the colonies in America and the West Indies.

In the early months of 1749 he fell into the company of John Brown, also known as Dawson, who earned his living as a highwayman and robber. Brown and Poulter became the leaders of a gang that robbed houses across the nation, moving from town to town as suspicion fell on them. In Chester,

Poulter acquired, through a robbery, a fine roll of material fit to make a jacket for the best of gentry. Not one to hide his light under a bushel, he called a tailor to the Black Dog Inn where he was staying and described how he wanted his new garment to look. Put simply, it was loud and garish, well over the top and clearly Poulter's way of showing how successful he had become. It was a villain's boastful expression of himself and the tailor's suspicions were confirmed as he attempted to take a waist measurement and the loaded pistol tucked in Poulter's belt was accidentally fired. The bullet mercifully passed through the ceiling. The tailor reported the matter to the mayor but by the time the alarm had been raised, Poulter and his gang were already on their way across the Irish Sea. Continuing his life of crime, his gang travelled around Ireland. Eventually Poulter tried unsuccessfully to settle down to an honest life as a publican but he was obliged to make a hasty return to England, having been betrayed by his former companions when he refused to rejoin them in their life of crime.

It is at this point that Poulter established his links with Somerset. Having teamed up with two other criminals, Dick Branning and John Roberts, his newly-formed gang set up their headquarters in Bath. From there, they embarked on a career of highway robbery, roaming far and wide. Trowbridge, Halifax, Chester, Manchester, Grantham, Nottingham, Durham and Newcastle all fell victim to the gang's highway activities. Every now and again, they would return to their Bath headquarters, at least until the heat died down. They then turned their attentions to the South-West, staying closer to home, striking in North Devon and Exeter before returning once more to Bath. Then back up north, concentrating on the series of horse fairs and other such events until returning once more to John Roberts' Bath abode.

It then became apparent that a number of locals were beginning to hold them in suspicion. Their way of dress, their apparent abundance of money and their frequent disappearances coincided with highway robberies across the country. To counter this, they 'leaked' the news that they were actually smugglers. Duties on imports such as tea and cloth were so high that everybody loved a smuggler. To complete the illusion, they would actually buy tea at the full price only to sell it at a fraction of the cost.

Every once in a while, they would change the nature of the crime and for a time attended fairs around the county, picking pockets and lifting purses where crowds hustled around wrestlers or the cock-fighting, or buying horses with false monetary promises. Further excursions into Dorset, Berkshire and Bristol were followed by another retreat to count their spoils back in Bath.

Soon after this, Poulter led an attack on a horse-drawn coach near the Somerset border on the road to Trowbridge. Within the coach were a Dr Hancock and his young daughter. Poulter led the attack and in forcing his hand through the window, badly cut his wrist and in the process accidentally fired his pistol. A new recruit to the crew, believing the battle had started, responded by firing his own pistol, both bullets passing harmlessly through the carriage. The young girl was terrified but Poulter picked her up and kissed her, promising that no one would come to any harm. The doctor was robbed of his money, a gold watch and an amount of clothing. It was a poor reward for a robbery that was to prove so costly for Poulter.

The gang headed for a nearby inn where such villains were welcome. In fact, the landlord kindly melted down a couple of spoons to make pistol balls to replace those used in the robbery. Fed and watered, and with their munitions replenished, they headed out of the area as fast as they could to avoid detection, arriving in Exeter where the stolen goods were exchanged for cash. However, the law finally caught up with them.

Just three weeks later, after a very full life of crime, Poulter was arrested under suspicion of the robbery of Dr Hancock. Held in Ilchester gaol, his trial was a formality and he was condemned to death. In confessing his crimes, and in the hope of a reprieve, he named more than thirty of his former associates, also providing all the information the authorities needed with regard to meeting places and hide-outs. Somehow word leaked out of the names listed, or perhaps his former associates had already drawn the conclusion that Poulter would betray them. By the time the authorities set about their series of arrests, only twelve of those listed could be found. His list of confessions was so long that it was actually published as a book and remained a best seller for years afterwards.

Meanwhile, Dr Hancock's property had been found and returned, but the fact that Poulter had received the death penalty clearly did not satisfy him. He wanted it to be sooner rather than later and endeavoured to make that happen. He actually visited Poulter in Ilchester gaol and told him that he would do his best to get the highwayman pardoned. But outside, Hancock was playing a different game, doing everything in his power to expedite the execution.

Poulter's execution had been postponed for six weeks, partly because of his confession but more importantly because he was required as a witness in the trials of those he had betrayed. So many villains were brought to justice that gentlemen from across the West Country petitioned for his pardon, the instigators of crimes against them now being in the hands of the law. But the gaoler felt no compassion for Poulter and treated him most cruelly. It is therefore not surprising that Poulter, assisted by another prisoner, forced the bars on his cell window and escaped. Through the night and with their legs in irons, they walked the byways of Somerset, hoping to head for Wales. In Glastonbury they managed to get their irons removed and then laid up for the day in a hayrick. As night fell on their second day they headed up towards the Mendip Hills and the village of Wookey. Poulter was in a very poor condition, exhausted from his treatment in gaol. His legs and ankles were raw from the chafing of the irons. He desperately needed to rest and unwisely went to an alehouse where he was soon recognised and recaptured.

Back in Ilchester gaol, he still had nine days until his execution. However, such was the concern that he might escape again, the execution was brought forward and before the day was out, Poulter was taken from his cell and hanged. It was 25th February 1755 and the life and career of one of Somerset's most prolific highwaymen had come to an end.

Into the 19th century

Although highway robbery peaked in the 18th century, it was to continue unabated into the next century. Isaac Milsom was found guilty at the Somerset Assizes in March 1825 and his death penalty was repealed to fourteen years' transportation to Australia. Just six years later, two brothers from Bathampton were to suffer the same fate. William Austin, a kitchen gardener, and his younger brother James, aged 21, were put on trial at the Bridgwater Assizes for highway robbery and initially received a death sentence, which was then commuted to transportation for life. In August 1831, they sailed for Australia aboard the *Strathfieldsay*, arriving mid-November. Ten years later, William married Helen McIntosh and raised a family in Tasmania.

Thomas Kidner and Charles Collard, highwaymen

Much better documented are the tales of Thomas Kidner and his accomplice Charles Collard. Charles was born in North Petherton in 1811, the son of Richard and Peggy Collard, and was baptised in the parish church. It would seem that the family were God-fearing people, his father being the church sexton. Charles was the sixth of the family of eight children, having six sisters and a brother. By the time he was aged 21 he was working as a shoemaker with a younger lad, Thomas Kidner, aged 17. The two of them took to crime and were eventually caught for highway robbery and assault.

Early in 1832, they attacked, assaulted and robbed William Lally, stealing four pairs of stockings and about five shillings in cash. Lally was on his way home to Taunton from Bridgwater market with his wife. Less than a mile outside North Petherton, at 11 o'clock in the morning, Collard punched Lally in the mouth and then knocked him unconscious with a stick. He remained unconscious until 4 o'clock the following morning.

At their trial, Charles Collard stood before the bench, charged with highway robbery, sporting bright red hair and whiskers, and adorned with a multitude of tattoos. As the case against them was presented, Collard threw a fit and had to be removed. They were both found guilty. Charles could already boast previous offences, one just three years earlier that had earned him a whipping at the post and two months in Wilton gaol in Taunton for stealing two pairs of shoes.

The death sentence was announced in both cases but commuted to transportation for life for Collard and two years hard labour for Kidner. After passing time in Ilchester gaol, by mid-September Collard was aboard a

Charles and Mary Collard. Courtesy of their great-great-grandson, William Bell, Melbourne, Australia.

North Petherton's Charles Collard in Eddington Cemetery, Victoria, Australia – transported but not forgotten.

prison hulk at Woolwich, bound for Van Diemen's Land on the *Emperor Alexander*, arriving in August 1833. Eight years later, in 1841, he was granted a conditional pardon and given his ticket to leave. This meant he was free to go wherever he wished except back home to Britain or Ireland.

During his time as a convict, he had worked for one George Allan who had met a Mary McLean on her voyage to Australia. She had travelled by assisted passage as a free woman from Perthshire and George Allan appears to have recruited her as a maidservant. That was how Charles Collard met Mary McLean. They married and started a family. Around 1850 and 1851, they travelled to California at the time of the gold diggings there but did not accrue the wealth they had hoped for; indeed they experienced a series of dreadful fires and earthquakes. They returned to Australia, with their first three children in tow, to purchase a farm at Baringhup, West Victoria, which is where Charles spent the remainder of his days. A further child was added to the family, a son called Daniel who was born in a tent, and whose great-great-grandson William Bell kindly provided this information.

Charles Collard suffered from poor physical health during his last five years, subsequent to a stroke. He died of influenza in September 1891, leaving a widow, four grown-up children and 27 grandchildren.

7

FORGERY, UTTERANCE AND COINING

It is fascinating to reflect on how attitudes have changed with regard to crimes related to our financial systems. It is possible today to defraud a company or community to the tune of billions and at worst receive a prison sentence. Historically, you risked the death penalty just for clipping the edge from a coin. This practice was termed 'coining' and was a capital offence because of the intent behind it. Coins once were made of gold or silver and by clipping a bit off each of several coins, sufficient precious metal could be acquired to produce new counterfeit ones. Forgery has long been a crime and one that we still recognise today, but 'utterance' is perhaps a term with which we are not so familiar. It is simply the criminal act of passing a counterfeit note, coin or document. It was another offence that at one time could lead to the hangman's noose.

Imagine a situation where you walk into a public bar. You order a round of drinks, offer a £10 note to pay for them, the barman passes the note under an ultra-violet scanner and detects that the note is a forgery. It's a common experience and we all know someone who has inadvertently fallen victim to this. But imagine, in that same scenario, that the barman then calls the police and you find yourself arrested, subsequently facing the death penalty. Just being in possession of such a forgery could result in fourteen years' transportation at best. How times have changed. The apparently respectable Ennever family of Bath got caught up in this in the early 19th century – but on reflection they may not have been totally innocent.

The Ennever family affair

John and Sarah Ennever of Bath had married in 1782 and raised a family of four sons and three daughters. Outwardly the family appeared well dressed, well mannered and law-abiding, but things began to go wrong one day in January 1807 when Joseph, the second son, who worked as a shoemaker, became involved in the distribution of forged banknotes. Joseph was out for the day with his brother George and a woman called Mary Radford. George and Mary had lived together in Birmingham and it would appear that, whilst there, they had become acquainted with a gang of forgers. Just before

Christmas, Mary had returned to Birmingham with £10 to buy £50 worth of forgeries. On the day they were caught red-handed, it was Mary who tried to pass a forged note during a transaction. The forgery was spotted and an attempt made to apprehend all three of them. George managed to escape but Joseph and Mary were arrested.

Mary, being interviewed, spilled the beans, effectively turning King's evidence and thereby saving her own neck. No charges were brought against her. The Bank of England was notified and they instructed that Joseph should be tried for the capital offences of forging and passing the counterfeit notes. Joseph was tried at Taunton Castle, where he protested his innocence, arguing, and maybe correctly, that it was his brother George and Mary who were at fault. He was found guilty and condemned to death by hanging. The court made a point of expressing their satisfaction that Joseph's parents, John and Sarah, were considered to be blameless in this whole affair, simply living innocently under the same roof.

On 22nd April, alongside a fellow prisoner about to suffer the same fate, 23-year-old Joseph was taken to Gallows Field, close to Ilchester gaol where he had been held. As was usual for such occasions, a large jeering and taunting crowd of people were gathered awaiting the day's entertainment. After the execution, Joseph's family were able to reclaim his body, which was buried in Weston Cemetery, Bath.

Meanwhile, back in Bath, the shopkeeper and police involved in the arrest and prosecution shared the £50 reward, which was the accepted payout made by the Bank of England. Mary Radford, who was the one who had bought the forgeries in the first place, not only got away without a prosecution but also received 26 guineas to cover her reward and cost of lodgings during the trial.

But let's not forget George, who managed to escape the whole affair. He fled and hid in London until the heat had died down. He was soon followed by his parents, John and Sarah, who by now had changed their name to Morris. Within two years, Sarah was caught red-handed, passing a forged £2 note in payment for 5 shillings' worth of goods. At her trial, she appeared the complete picture of innocence and no one had any idea that she might have had previous connections with her sons' criminal activities. She was found not guilty.

George, however, continued his life of crime, narrowly escaping capture in London when a fellow villain named all of his criminal associates in order to save his own neck. George had to make a quick exit and there then followed a series of petty crimes across the country until inevitably he was caught once again in the act of forgery. Tried and found guilty, he was lucky to escape with transportation to Australia. By turning King's evidence, he persuaded the authorities to allow his wife, Ann, and his children to be transported with him to Australia, to which in the coming months he was followed by a whole convoy of other villains, all of whom he had named. He was also joined several years after that by his brother William who clearly had chosen a similar career path.

8

DAYS OF SMUGGLING

---- ❋ ----

During the 17th and 18th centuries, thanks to the punitive expense of various wars, high taxes were imposed on many imported items. The additional cost was indeed so high that it positively encouraged the activity of smugglers who could make a lucrative trade if not caught. But smuggling was a problem well before those days.

The smuggling vicar
Bridgwater can boast some of the earliest records available of the evasion of customs duty. The Borough Court documents for April 1380 show that John Cole, a merchant of the town, was found to have:

> ... held back and concealed by his trickery and subtlety the lord's customs of corn sold to foreign merchants in the harbour of Bridgwater during 12 years, to wit, 10,000 quarters of corn, in deception of lord and lordship of Bridgwater reaching the sum of £20. And that J.C. in the same manner for the whole time aforesaid withdrew the customs of the lord and lordship of iron, fish, salt, wine and other merchandise sold to divers foreign merchants.

Shortly after, there was another court case concerning yet more individuals who would deprive the lord of his duties. In this case the miscreants had persuaded a ship from Ilfracombe to dock at Combwich where they could unload its cargo of herrings without paying duty; likewise a ship from Tenby, a Cornish vessel and a barge, which were laden with salt and corn. The villains were found guilty with damages of £100. What was particularly of interest was not just that two of the group were Bridgwater burgesses, but that the third member of this band of smugglers was the vicar of Otterhampton!

Bridgwater's duty officers
In the early decades of the 16th century, the shipping trade appeared to have gone into decline, being half of its former volume by 1550. There was no apparent reason for this decline and it would suggest that the full extent of

the trade was simply not being recorded, in other words there was extensive smuggling going on. Despite this, in 1565 a special commission reported:

> *Bridgwater is much frequented and haunted with traffic of merchants and merchandises to the inward and outward and it is to be continued for that purpose. There are no places or sellers, warehouses or store houses near unto the said port where lading or unloading is or hath been used whereby the Queen's Majesty is defrauded of her customs <u>as far as we know</u>.*

Bridgwater, as a port, had responsibility for collecting duty on most types of imports even as far along the coast as Minehead. The duty officer had considerable distances to travel and, needless to say, when his back was turned there were those who would take advantage. Duty officer Daniel Yates complained that the ship *Encrease* from Virginia in June 1679 landed 60 hogsheads of tobacco before he had a chance to collect the duty, which he managed on the remaining 125 hogsheads. Duty could only be collected when he witnessed the unloading. One man, called George Atwell, reported that a wagonload of cloth, big enough that it took twelve oxen to pull it, had escaped his attention.

The government sent in two investigators, William Culliford and Arnold Browne. Between them they gained confessions to 101 tuns of wine and brandy and 2,357 packages of linen having escaped duty during a three-year period. A search of the town turned up contraband all over the place. In their final report they referred to the customs' collector as dishonest and seldom if ever sober!

The West Somerset shoreline

The Quantock Hill village of Kilve lies close to the rocky shoreline at Kilve beach, a one-time favourite haunt of smugglers. Between the village and the shore will be found the ruins of Kilve Priory, a relic from medieval days. Having fallen into disrepair, it was used during the early 19th century as a storage depot for smugglers bringing in brandy under the noses of the excise men. However, in 1848 when the excise men got too close for comfort, it was realised that a raid on the secret store was imminent. The smugglers set fire to the brandy, which blew up, leaving the priory building in ruins – as we see it today. The problem of smuggling did not exactly go away. The tower of the 13th-century church was used instead.

Along the coast at Watchet, smuggling was just as rife. There were so many incidents in the 17th century that Charles ll sent his Surveyor-Governor to investigate. He soon realised that what had once been a poor community now flourished with new-found wealth. His report concluded that the smuggling activity was well established from as high as the Lord of the

Manor down to the lowliest mariner.

> *From being beggars within these ten years the whole town has grown exceeding rich and now have as great an overseas trade as Minehead ... At Watchet it was found that several small vessels had no other business but that of running goods, and that the collector of customs there usually sat drinking with the masters of ships while gangs of men were unloading them.*

William Dashwood was the collector of taxes and the report concluded that not only was he in league with the smugglers, but whenever you needed to find him he would be in one of the town's inns. Dashwood was suspended and his assistant Mr Perry, who had betrayed him, was promoted into his place. Perry immediately became the town's number one enemy and could include Sir William Wyndham, Lord of the Manor, amongst those whose wrath he had incurred.

Whilst a closer eye was kept on Watchet, the smugglers simply chose other places along the coastline to bring goods ashore, such as St Audries Bay and Blue Anchor where the Smugglers' Inn can be found. Beyond Minehead, which had fairly tight control of its imports, smuggling was also rife at Porlock and Porlock Weir. The Ship Inn at Porlock is famous for its smuggling links and just a little further along the coast is the tiny hamlet of Culbone, with its isolated chapel, the smallest in England. It was here that a community of lepers existed and the location was favoured by smugglers as a place to store contraband.

From the Brue to Bristol

Sand Point, projecting finger-like into the channel to the north of Weston-super-Mare, allowed good visibility for smugglers, and excise men could be spotted well before they arrived. From their high-up position, look-outs could direct the lighting of beacons to guide the smugglers' ships ashore. Similar signalling points existed at Uphill, where the church tower was used, and on Worlebury Hill.

Smugglers were pretty lucky in that they were seldom caught. Imprisonment with hard labour was the commonest punishment when they were, perhaps because the death penalty would have been socially unacceptable, smugglers being popular with people generally – unlike highwaymen – because they helped to keep down the cost of imports. Hard labour was the punishment received by Burnham-on-Sea's mariner Samuel Turner who was found guilty of smuggling in 1854. It was worse, however, for the ship owners who risked the confiscation of their vessels.

9
ILCHESTER GAOL

———— ✤ ————

The county gaol was located at Ilchester for nearly 600 years in total. As far back as 1166, the circuit courts were held there but in 1280 the court and gaol were moved to Somerton, the county's one-time capital, only to return in 1366. And that's where the gaol remained until 1843. It was the principal site for executions, which took place to the south of the town at Gallows Field, just to the west of the Yeovil road. There were even executions with burning at the stake, as dealt with in Chapter 4, a form of execution abolished in 1790. It is the 18th century, however, that is the best documented.

A report by a Dr Lettsom produced in 1807 described the layout of the gaol. It had 16-ft-high walls around its perimeter. The gaoler's house was placed centrally, next to the chapel and with its own vegetable garden. Around that and within the walls were five separate blocks, each with its own courtyard. Men and women were kept separate, as were the debtors and felons, who were kept away from the other criminals. The ground floor of the blocks provided open-sided shelter from the weather. On the first and second floors were the cells, reached by a stone staircase. These were about 9 ft by 6 ft, having an outer iron gate and inner wooden door. Overcrowding at times was so bad that the prisoners had to remove the roof tiles to get enough air to breathe. The beds were made of iron and the straw bedding could be changed once a month, for a fee. Regulation yellow and brown-striped prison shirts were free, but generally not used.

The busy days of the 18th century
Fairly accurate records exist for executions in the county during the 18th century, particularly for the latter 65 years. Extending these figures to 100 years, we can reasonably assume that during that century around 1,000 death sentences would have been pronounced in the county, so about ten per annum; of those around 270 would have been carried out, the remainder receiving the benefit of a reprieve, usually with the sentence downgraded to transportation. Overwhelmingly those executions were carried out on the Gallows Field at Ilchester. A limited number were carried out elsewhere, at least seven at Taunton, two each at Bridgwater and Bedminster Down, and

one each on Chilton Heath, Black Down, Odd Down at Bath, North Perrot, Dodwell Green near Kingston St Mary, Ilton and one burnt at the stake in Wells.

The court cases for these serious crimes were normally held at the quarterly assizes, generally the Lent Assizes being held in Taunton and the Summer Assizes in Bridgwater. Based on the years for which information is available, the rough breakdown of executions for each reason was as follows, averaging three per year:

Housebreaking and other theft	93
Murder	51
Highway robbery	47
Horse theft	37
Sheep and cattle theft	17
Counterfeiting, forgery etc	8
Rape	6
At large when in transportation	6
Riot	4
Sacrilege (presumably theft from a church)	1

One transgression that doesn't show up in this list is that of missing church on a Sunday. It was back in the 17th century that absence from Sunday service was a crime and it was a particular issue for Quakers who preferred to follow their own form of worship, but the law stated that it was the 'regular' church that had to be attended.

Joseph Scadding, keeper of Ilchester gaol, 1757 to 1771

In 1737 when Susannah Broom from Bridgwater married 23-year-old Joseph Scadding from Pitminster she could have had no idea that she would later become the gaoler's wife at the county gaol. Initially they lived in Pitminster, then Corfe, followed by Ilchester and during those years of marriage were blessed with twelve children. Joseph was a yeoman farmer and whilst living in Ilchester in 1757 accepted the role of county gaoler. Although one would expect such a position to provide a reasonable salary, it did not. Indeed, there was no pay at all but plenty of expenses. There were, however, ways to compensate.

The job came with its own family-sized accommodation, albeit attached to the gaol. It was a condition of his contract with the County Sheriff that he should be resident at the gaol. That same contract also required him to ensure that no one escaped, hence his first task was to take a list of the inmates at the time that he took over. This then had to be agreed with the Sheriff. He was also required to ensure that prisoners were taken to the courts at the required time and this was to be done at his own expense. He had to pay the executioner's fees and the cost of other forms of punishment unless he inflicted them himself. So how could he make an honest living from such a position? Simply put, he was allowed to take any fees, profits or advantages that he wanted in respect of the prisoners. Since the comfort and welfare of a prisoner depended on the quality of the food and drink received, and on any other privileges, it was essential to survival that the gaoler's palm be greased with compensation. It was a lucrative source of income, which came from those with the money. For the others, it was an overcrowded cell, shared beds and very poor food.

Joseph remained as the county gaoler until his death in 1771 when his eighth child, Edward, assumed the role.

Edward Scadding, keeper of Ilchester gaol, 1771 to 1808

At 17 years old, Edward left the family home at Ilchester gaol and travelled to London where he served a seven-year apprenticeship as a goldsmith. Within a few months of completing his indentures and taking up a permanent position in New Bond Street, his father died and Edward returned home where, rather surprisingly, he accepted the mantle of his father's former role, which would suggest that it was indeed a lucrative position. Eleven years later, now aged 36, he married Martha and this was to be another marriage blessed with twelve offspring.

It seems that by this time the lot of the gaoler had improved and a salary was being paid of £25 per annum. This income was then supplemented according to the type of prisoner held within:

Debtors	14s 4d
Felons	6s 8d
Transportees	£3 12s 0d

The records for 1774 show that the number of felons and debtors present would have provided additional income in excess of £54, plus the benefits from transportees and the keeper's profits from food, wine and liquor, all of which he was entitled to sell at inflated prices within the gaol. As the years passed, the salary increased to £125 and the compensation for felons doubled. Having once lived and worked in London, undoubtedly Edward would have enjoyed the opportunities to travel which came once in a while, taking prisoners to trial usually in Bridgwater or Taunton, but occasionally all the way to the capital city. No doubt many suffered at his hand, but no doubt many benefited from his care. At least one lady was appreciative, although it was only after her release that she truly realised how well Edward and his family had cared for her. She was a very special guest.

A very special guest

The lady concerned was Jane Leigh-Perrot, the aunt of the famous Jane Austen. Jane Leigh-Perrot was born in Barbados where her father was a barrister. Aged six, she was sent to a boarding school in England and stayed with her uncle, Sir Montague Cholmeley, when the school was out for the holidays. It was a very privileged upbringing. Aged 21, she met and married the wealthy James Leigh-Perrot and from thenceforth led a sociable life of independence and leisure, with homes in both Berkshire and Bath. James suffered from gout and it was convenient to take the waters there. Their residence was number one, The Paragon, a resplendent terraced property, and there they lived a life of luxury – well, most of the time.

In the autumn of 1799 Jane was arrested for shoplifting £1 worth of lace. Her substantial wealth would suggest there was absolutely no need to steal but she was nonetheless arrested and taken to prison at Ilchester. If found guilty, the penalty for the theft of any item valued at over a shilling was death commuted to transportation. It was a grim prospect for someone used to fine living. The shock of prison routine must have been horrific for her.

Despite her wealthy status, or perhaps because of it, she was refused bail. But at least her wealth could help to make prison life more tolerable by paying for the favours of the gaoler, Edward Scadding. Rather than incarceration in a cold prison cell, she was allowed to lodge with Scadding's family and it was there that her husband joined her for a period. Her letters home described the family of five young noisy children with three cats and two dogs as pets. The older children were more readily accepted especially since they entertained the lady musically. But it was little compensation for the smoke that blew down the chimney, the general cleanliness of the place falling below her high standards, and the children who licked their knives and spilt food and drink on her husband! And Edward Scadding swore a lot.

Despite these observations, she was nonetheless aware that her plight would have been far worse without the kindness of the Scadding family and she commented that it was not their fault that they had lower standards than herself. Very gracious of her! But there were additional benefits in staying with Edward's family. Many of his friends and relations were regular members of the jury and were always willing to follow his advice. Fortunately her discomfort was soon over and she was found not guilty at her trial in Taunton. The unfortunate episode had done nothing to harm her standing in social circles and within two years the Austen family had moved in with them prior to finding their own accommodation. Meanwhile, her husband kept an eye on her during her shopping expeditions.

Ten days after her release from prison, Jane wrote to Martha Scadding asking for an invoice for the services provided. This was to be the first of several letters, which showed that a real friendship had developed between the two ladies. Martha's reply was described as 'in the most elegant handwriting'. Enclosed with a chatty letter updating Jane on the family and the various inmates was an invoice for £2. Jane's response was to send a cheque for the value of £25, indicating just how appreciative she really was.

A lucky escape for Edward

In October 1786 Edward was lucky to escape what could have been a murderous attempt on his life or the life of his deputy. A gang of inmates had been provided with knives smuggled in by a horse-stealer. These were dangerous and murderous men. Their plan was to use the knives to free themselves from their chains, and then form up in a passageway to make their escape, the strongest at the front, the weakest to the rear. However, the plan needed to be delayed when it was realised that, with Edward attending the assizes at Taunton, Pitman (his deputy) and another helper were in a room overlooking the yard across which they would need to pass. This would put them in the line of fire of the rifles that were held in the deputy's room. At least half of them could expect to die – but as some of them commented, they had nothing to lose. The plot was postponed and in the meantime two of the less courageous members of the gang lost their confidence and reported the planned attempt.

First offenders

Whilst modern-day practice is to be lenient and understanding towards first offenders, this was not the case in the days of yesteryear as was demonstrated in the case of Robert Dallamont and Elias Peach, two young lads aged just 19 and 21. The following report from the *Western Gazette* of April 1790 provides some of the detail:

> *Wednesday se'nnight were executed at Ilchester, pursuant to their sentence at last Taunton assizes, Elias Peach and Robert Dallamont, alias Gillam, for house-breaking. They appeared very penitent. After hanging the usual time, their bodies were put into the coffins on which they sat in the cart to the place of execution, and delivered to their friends for burial.*
>
> *Elias Peach was only 21. After having travelled to Newfoundland, Spain, Portugal and Italy, being out of employ went to Poole to ship himself again for Newfoundland, but not succeeding, was returning from Poole on the 28th of February last, when he met with Dallamont at Bere who was going to Poole on the same errand; but finding he had not succeeded, they agreed to return and employ themselves in plundering. The first object they met with near Dorchester was a genteel lad about 14, with a watch in his pocket: Dallamont was for robbing him, but being so near the town and some persons appearing at the time, Peach's heart failed him, and the lad escaped. They went on for*

Frampton, and meeting a miller with a leather pouch slung over his shoulder, they agreed to attack him, but Peach's heart failed him a second time, saying the country was open, they should be pursued and taken. Dallamont being angry with Peach for disappointing him again, they had some words before Peach could be pacified: Peach then said, d_ _n thee let's go home and rob old Gibbs, he having more money than he can tell what to do with; for which robbery they both suffered.

Robert Dallamont, aged 19, was born at Hardington and said the plundering (of) Mr Gibbs' house was the first offence he had ever committed. They cautioned all young people to take warning as keeping bad company was their ruin.

Little change in the 19th century

The 19th century saw little change in the pace of executions, which still averaged three per year. Theft in its various forms remained the most popular, whilst forgery and its related crimes (utterance, coining) rose to the number three spot, murder slipping to fourth position. A summary of the first two decades of executions is as follows:

Housebreaking and other theft	21
Highway robbery	8
Counterfeiting, forgery etc	8
Murder	7
Sheep and cattle theft	7
Horse theft	4
Assault	2
Rape	1
Bestiality	1

The single rape case mentioned here was a particularly horrific one where James Gardner raped 7-year-old Kezia Gould in one of Somerset's earliest recorded cases of paedophilia. Gardner was hanged in Ilchester gaol on 11th September 1816.

Mr Bridle, the new keeper

On the retirement of Edward Scadding, a new keeper was appointed, Mr Bridle. In the years to come, he was to be the subject of a series of complaints regarding his cruel treatment of the prisoners. Questions were even raised in Parliament but it was pointed out that the manner in which a prison was kept was not a matter for government, but for the local sheriff in whom they should have complete confidence. The name of Bridle crops up in many reports from around that period, including that of the thief Arthur Bailey whose story is told later.

A privileged prisoner's view of prison life

In 1819 Ilchester gaol was to receive one of its wealthiest and most influential inmates, Henry 'Orator' Hunt, a politician and radical. He had been invited to address a gathering of around 800 people in Manchester at an event that was to be attacked by the police, resulting in eleven deaths. Henry Hunt was tried for attempting to cause a riot and sentenced to two and a half years in Ilchester gaol. During his time there, he wrote copiously about his life inside, well – almost inside. With money, you could buy anything and here we can discover just how great the opportunities were for the gaoler to earn a small fortune. Describing his arrival, Hunt wrote:

> I arrived at the prison about two o'clock, and was conducted into the coffee room, kept by Mr. Davey, the Marshal's coachman, where we were soon accommodated with a very good dinner. In the mean time I had made the necessary inquiry for an apartment, but the prison was represented to be very full; and I was shewn one or two rooms, where the parties occupying them had no objection to turn out, to accommodate me, for a certain stipulated sum. Amongst the number I was shewn up into a very good room, which was occupied by a lady, who, it was said, would give up her room for ten pounds. When we entered the room she was singing very divinely, she being no less a personage than Mrs. Wells, the celebrated public singer.
>
> With great freedom she inquired which was the gentleman, me or my attorney, who accompanied me; and upon being informed that I was the prisoner, she eyed me over from head to toe, and then, with that art of which she was so much a mistress, she simpering said, that 'she was loath to part with her room at any price, but that, as I appeared a nice wholesome country gentleman, I should be welcome to half of it without paying any thing.' As I was not prepared to enter into a contract of that sort, I hastily retired, and left my attorney to settle the quantum of pecuniary remuneration with her.

His account continues with a description of six of them enjoying a sumptuous meal, complete with tablecloth, after which he was visited by two local vicars. During their conversations, he explained his predicament to one of the parsons, as to how it was impossible to find a suitable room. The parson took up his case and went to negotiate with the gaoler and then the marshal, who, apart from acting for the circuit judge in his absence, was his close friend and neighbour. The vicar soon returned with a flea in his ear having been told that such arrangements were not in the line of duty of a parson, he would only negotiate with Hunt's attorney. Within ten minutes the matter was settled. Henry Hunt would have an apartment over the lobby of the gaol. For this he would be given a key and would be able to have access to the outside world. He would be all but free. However, a bond of £5,000 had to be paid against his escape and a significant amount paid to the marshal and the gaoler. Henry Hunt was delighted with the arrangement. He was in prison on the outside! He described his feelings at that moment:

I returned to my friends elated with the prospect of my being so comfortable, as I had been very much disgusted with the scenes of profligacy and drunkenness that I had already witnessed within the walls. Mrs. Filewood, the principal turnkey's wife, who kept the lobby, was to prepare my bed, and get every thing ready for me in my room by ten o'clock, the time at which my friends were to leave the prison. When the hour arrived, I was shown into a very spacious room, nicely furnished, with a neat bureau bedstead, standing in one corner. My hostess, who was a pretty, modest-looking woman, was very communicative, and so attentive that I really felt quite as comfortable as if I had been at an inn. It was, in fact, much better than the apartments I had been in at the inn, in London, the Black Lion, Water Lane. There was a good fire in the room, and every thing bore the air of cleanliness and comfort, and I went to bed and slept till day-light, as sound and as well as I ever slept in my life.

The following morning, Hunt regretted not having made enquiries of another well-to-do gentleman, Mr Waddington, whom he understood was also residing there at His Majesty's pleasure. But he was not to wait for long. His hostess tapped on his door to announce that Mr Waddington had requested the pleasure of his company for breakfast and was awaiting him in the apartment immediately above Hunt's. For the next six weeks, they dined together, Mrs Davey, the coachman's wife providing the catering. Thereafter, many an evening was spent deep in conversation about political affairs, often with their respective attorneys joining them. It was almost like a holiday!

As Christmas approached, Hunt and Waddington never shirked their duties as benefactors, ensuring ample Christmas boxes were provided not just for their staff back in their respective homes, but also for those who saw to their needs in the gaol, and those poor distressed characters within the prison walls. On visiting the less fortunate inmates, they discovered some naked of both clothing and bedding and some pining away to a state of wretchedness. They did everything they could to reduce the suffering through the assistance of the marshal.

They were also to discover how some of the prisoners had suffered at the hands of the turnkeys. Asking why an inmate had not complained to the magistrate, the prisoner looked long and hard at Hunt, wondering what kind of fool would ask such a question and replied:

Lord, Sir! you will know better after you have been here a little while. I have been here nearly two years, and I never knew any prisoner make a complaint even to the gaoler, and much less to the magistrate, without being punished for it. I never knew a man make a complaint who was not locked up, in solitary confinement, within a week afterwards, for something or other. A prisoner is sure never to get any redress, for the turnkeys will say anything, and what one says another will swear; and the gaoler always believes them, or pretends to believe them, in preference to the prisoners; so do what they will with us, we never complain.

The ins and outs of prison life

There were very clearly two categories of prisoners, the haves and have nots, and occasionally someone who fitted in between. Such was the case with a particularly refined lady and her daughter who had been committed to the prison for debt. Learning of their arrival, Hunt and Waddington made a point of inviting them to dinner. The invitation was accepted but an immediate problem was identified. Hunt and Waddington were effectively outside the prison but allowed in, whereas the ladies were within but not allowed out. Hunt went to see the marshal, the only person with the power to change the situation. The marshal, in turn, enquired of his turnkey as to what the level of debt was and, being told it was £300, asked Hunt if he would stand surety for that amount. When Hunt asked if that was acceptable, the marshal replied: 'Your word, Mr. Hunt, is quite sufficient.' He then faced the turnkey and said, 'Recollect, sir, that Mrs. M—e and her daughter have free access to Mr. Hunt's and Mr. Waddington's apartments, to dine, drink tea, and spend the evening whenever they please to invite them; and take care also that they have a good room provided for them, if they have not already got such within the walls.'

An account such as this can make prison life sound quite tolerable. It wasn't. Hunt and others like him were very much the exception. Within the walls, prisoners suffered horrifically, and for many of them it was a case of watching the days tick by until their execution. But the situation was slowly improving, thanks to the watchful eye of a committee. In an 1823 report by the Committee of the Society for the Improvement of Prisons, Ilchester was described as providing instructions each morning for the prisoners in how to read. The lessons were organised by the prison chaplain who would select instructors from among those in prison as debtors. At other times the prisoners were employed in making shoes and clothes for the inmates of various prisons, breaking stones (hard labour) and in building work within the prison. The committee were pleased to report that the governor had ceased the practice of keeping prisoners in irons.

Such a minor offence

When a family is starving, it can be necessary for the father to make one of those life and death decisions. The choice is to watch his family starve or to steal food and run the risk of capture and probable death by hanging. That was the quandary faced by Amos Plummer who lived with his young family at Kilmersdon. Amos had only been married for five years. He was captured when robbing a tailor and confessed to petty thefts from fishponds and milk houses in dairies, and to stealing potatoes. These strongly suggest that the family were desperate for food. But no mercy was shown at his trial and he was hanged at Ilchester Gallows Field in April 1801.

A family affair

Although the Caines family lived at Oldland Common near Bitton, which is just in Gloucestershire, their escapades took them into the surrounding counties and hence into Somerset when Francis Caines unwisely decided to cross the border. But first, let's look at the family background. In 1727 Abraham Caines found himself in prison. In 1763 his son Benjamin inherited his father's role as the patriarch of a family of criminals. At least four of Benjamin's sons and a daughter were to fall foul of the law:

George	Transported for life
Francis	Hanged at Ilchester gaol
Betty	Transported
Thomas	Transported
Benjamin	Hanged

It was a truly villainous family with Benjamin, the father of this group, looked upon as a latter-day 'Godfather'. But our story here focuses on the activity and subsequent execution in Somerset of the second son, Francis, described in the prison record as an 'oyster and cider seller'.

It was 11th May 1804. Francis Caines was a member of a gang led by Thomas Batt and which included Charles (alias The Squire) Fuller and John Manners, all from Bitton. A few days before their planned and fateful raid, Charles Fuller rode to Bath and there he hired a coach house, not far from Pulteney Street. On the evening of the raid, the gang of four ate and drank well at a hostelry in Bath. Leaving at about 10 pm, they headed for Bathwick, and in a similar fashion to modern-day criminals who steal a car before raiding a bank or commercial premises, they broke into a stables and stole a horse and cart.

By midnight they had reached their destination, a store in Freshford village, owned by Thomas and Harry Joyce where they knew there was cloth valued at £450. They gained entry by simply smashing their way in and immediately set about loading the cart. A swift gallop away from Freshford brought them back to Bath at about 2 o'clock in the morning when they hid the horse, cart and load of cloth in the previously hired coach house. A man named Robert Bull had already been lined up to receive and dispose of the stolen goods.

Somehow they were discovered and Fuller, Caines and Manners were all arrested. It would appear that the gang leader, Thomas Batt, evaded capture and I have found no record of his trial or execution, albeit some accounts claim that he was tried and hanged at the same time as the rest of the gang. At their trial at the Summer Assizes in Wells, evidence against them poured in from the licensee of the Pulteney Arms inn, where they had been drinking, from bystanders who had seen their activity in the Pulteney Street area, from the turnpike man on the road from Freshford, from the stableman, coachman et cetera.

The outcome of the trial was inevitable. All were found guilty and condemned to death. Francis, in an unsuccessful attempt to achieve clemency, confessed his part in the crime. Fuller likewise gave evidence that led to the retrieval of the stolen cloth and identified Thomas Batt as the principal offender. No mercy was shown. All three were hanged at Ilchester's Gallows Field, Caines and Manners on 5th September 1804, Fuller just twelve days later, having been temporarily spared to provide evidence at other trials of those he had betrayed in attempts to save his own neck.

Arthur Bailey and Ilchester's last public execution

Arthur Bailey worked for the Post Office in Bath and gave all the appearances of an upright and honest man, doing his best to raise a respectable family. But behind the innocent façade, over the years he had stolen certain letters containing bills and other financial papers that he would be able to use to his advantage. Inevitably his dishonesty was detected and he was convicted of his crime and sentenced to death. With the death penalty hanging over him, his only chance stood in showing true remorse by confessing all the dishonest acts he had performed and by implicating anyone else involved. He denied any other crimes other than the one for which he was convicted and claimed that no other person had played any part.

Once incarcerated in Ilchester gaol, he was questioned by Mr Bridle, the keeper, who presented him with a list of other items missing from Bath post office. Initially he denied any knowledge of any of the missing items. Later he was to hear that his appeal for a reprieve had been turned down by the Secretary of State and the Postmaster-General. He made one more attempt for clemency by admitting to one item on the list being his responsibility, but he was not prepared to state which one. It could be assumed either that he had a bad memory or he was perhaps innocent of the other items, and hence would confess to one to save himself but not commit to which one in case questioning revealed that he was making up the story.

Whatever the reason, there was to be no reprieve. The fateful day came on 11th September 1811 and Arthur Bailey bade an emotional farewell to his wife and six children. The cart arrived to deliver him to the gallows. Once again, he was asked to confess the other crimes. He replied, 'I am about to suffer for what has been truly proved against me. All the rest must die with me.' He rode in the cart accompanied by the Under-Sheriff for the county and with the parson following in a chaise. He held himself firmly as the appointed hour approached. Beneath the gallows he shared a prayer and then addressed the audience with the Bible clenched in his hand: 'I hope you will all take warning. I beg you to look often into this book, and you will not come to shame. Be sure to be honest, and not covet money, cursed money! – and particularly money that is not your own.' The cart was then pulled away and he dropped to meet his maker. This was to be the last public execution carried out at the Gallows Field. Thereafter they were performed within the confines of the prison with the exception of those still carried out at the scenes of crimes elsewhere in the county.

Ilchester's final execution

The executions continued well into the 19th century but at least now no longer as a public spectacle. They continued to be for a wide range of crimes, not just murder. William Sage, aged 32, from Priddy on the Mendip Hills was a sheep stealer who, having stolen seven sheep, the property of a Mr Tudway, was perhaps aiming not just to feed his family but was more seriously involved. He was hanged on 28th April 1819 and, although having shown great repentance, received no mercy from the judge. Just a few months later, Charles Hibbert, a 59-year-old engraver from Walcot, near Bath received the same treatment for forgery.

In September 1839 Mr Justice Coleridge was presiding over the assizes at Bridgwater and he was clearly having a bad day. He had been so emotionally affected by one of the cases before him that he left the court room in tears. The accused had confessed to murder and that, whatever the circumstances, dictated that the judge had to pronounce the death sentence, a task which clearly affected him deeply.

Next to take the stand on that same day was 29-year-old Charles Wakeley who worked on a farm at Worle, near Weston-super-Mare. There, when he was supposed to be milking cows with 16-year-old Elizabeth Payne, his carnal desires got the better of him. She rebutted his sexual advances and angered him so much that he attacked her with a knife and killed her. Sentenced to be hanged, his execution took place at Ilchester gaol and proved to be the final execution in the town.

10

HANGING DAYS

———— ✳ ————

In May 1868, Parliament passed the Capital Punishment (Amendment) Act which ended the practice of holding executions in public view and required them to be carried out behind prison walls. However, the act allowed for the county sheriff to admit newspaper reporters and other witnesses, including the victim's relatives to the hanging. These public executions were also frequently held at the place of the crime, which in the majority of cases was on the home patch of the culprit of the crime. There was a two-fold purpose to these local and very public executions. Firstly, and perhaps most importantly, it provided a deterrent to the onlooker, aware of the painful death they could expect to meet should they commit some misdemeanour. Hangings were frequently followed by a period where the body, in chains and perhaps in a metal cage, would be left suspended from the gibbet for months to come, prolonging the period of 'education'. Secondly, and perhaps less importantly, they provided a great day out for those who enjoyed such events, the local population often being given time off work to enjoy what became known as 'hanging days' or 'hanging fairs' where wrestling, cock fighting and other diversions added to the spectacle.

These days were good for business. Drawing in such large crowds provided an opportunity for tradesmen to sell their wares, and it was also good for the landlords of some of the public houses along the route. It was not uncommon for the execution parties, who often had long distances to travel from the gaol to the place of execution, to stop at certain ale houses on the way. It would be known in advance which inns were to be used and it was the custom that the condemned prisoner be provided with a free jug of ale. Whilst this may seem generous on the part of the landlord, it was a small price compared with the huge amount of trade it brought in. And it also provides us with the origin of the expression 'One for the road', which was the phrase used by landlords just before they jokingly commented that the prisoner could pay for it on his way back!

Richard Biggs, hanging at Odd Down

An example of this, both in terms of the agony of the punishment and the ecstasy of the entertainment, is provided by the case of Richard Biggs. On

14th September 1748, Richard Biggs was executed on Odd Down, about a mile from Bath, in sight of the house where he lived and where the crime was committed. The following is an extract from the *General Advertiser* of 20th September:

Last Wednesday Richard Biggs, for the murder of his wife, was executed on Odd-Down, about a mile from Bath, in sight of the house where he liv'd, and was afterwards hung in chains. A vast multitude of people attended his execution. During his confinement in Ilchester Gaol, he behaved in a very sullen manner, regardless of death, but troubled at the thoughts of being hung in chains; for when the smith went to the Gaol to measure him, in order to make his irons, he flew in a passion, and refus'd him. – The manner of murdering his wife appears very shocking, her head, breast, arms, legs, and thighs, were covered all over with bruises, and wounds; and her lower parts greatly swelled black; and after exercising this cruelty, he flung her dead body into the river near Bath.

A week later, the same publication reported as follows:

We have this to add, relating to the execution of Richard Biggs, last Wednesday se'nnight, that after he had been on the ladder a short time, the Hangman attempted to fix the rope about his neck; when on a sudden he came down, and threw himself upon the ground, where he lay in a helpless manner. As it would have been a difficult matter to have got him up the ladder again; so it was judged proper to tie the rope to one of the rungs; and he was put on a horse's back, and from thence dragged off. – As he hung very low, he could not easily be seen; which was a disappointment to, perhaps, twenty thousand spectators, that came a great many miles to see him suffer. – When dead, his body was put in irons, and fixed on the gibbet: His behaviour all along was very sullen. – He was about 32 years of age.

We can judge from this description the unbelievable horror faced by the victim prior to such an execution and can see therein the impact it must surely have had on any onlookers. We can also see how there was significant importance in ensuring a good view of the proceedings when 20,000 spectators groaned in disappointment that the body was not sufficiently elevated for their benefit. With such large crowds, there was clearly a need to maintain good control at the event. The transport of the prisoner to the place of execution would be in the company of the County Sheriff or Under-Sheriff, the priest, hangman and a troop of javelin men, who carried military lances, to ensure that no public disorder broke out, nor any attempt to free the prisoner.

Jack White's Gibbet

Wincanton-born Jack White was still only 8 years old when his mother passed away. In 1716, by then aged 28, he was a hardened drinker, gambling man and married to Sarah Slade. Robert Sutton, a stranger to the area, entered the Sun Inn for food and drink. Jack White was already there and turned his attention to the stranger, who explained that he had a local delivery to complete. Jack offered to act as his guide and off they went. Having travelled some distance in the Bratton Seymour direction in scorching heat, they rested at the roadside and both were soon asleep.

Jack awoke in an ill temper and still drunk, just as two ladies were passing, going in the opposite direction. Jack crudely assaulted them and Robert Sutton woke up on hearing their screams. Realising what was happening, he leapt to the ladies' defence, but still had need of Jack's local knowledge. The ladies made their escape and the two men continued their journey. When Sutton was unaware of the danger, Jack White took his revenge and knocked him out, dislodging one of his eyes in the process, and then ran a stake into his mouth and out through his neck. Attempts to hide the body were unsuccessful and, on its discovery, the local community set about trying to discover the perpetrator of this evil deed.

Jack White was brought to trial, first before the Henstridge magistrate and then at the Bridgwater Assizes. Found guilty, he was hanged at the scene of the crime on 19th August 1730 and his body left to rot in a metal cage suspended from the gibbet. Over a hundred years later, in 1840, the gibbet was finally removed but the road junction still bears the name of 'Jack White's Gibbet'.

John Walford, Nether Stowey

Perhaps one of Somerset's most tragic stories is that of John Walford, a usually quiet and gentle giant, driven to despair. This led to the death of his wife and a very public execution. Cruelly, the gibbet on which his remains hung was in full view of his mother's front door. It is also a murder that has given us two landmark place names, Dead Woman's Ditch and Walford's Gibbet.

John Walford's existence was that of a charcoal burner on the Quantock Hills just above the village of Nether Stowey. It was lonely because the charcoal burner's fires had to be tended continuously, allowing no time for a social life. Hence for six days a week, John would gather the timber, then make and tend the slow-burning fires. Sundays were his only days off and he would visit his mother and girlfriend, Ann Rice, the miller's daughter.

Jane Shorney was the daughter of another charcoal burner and during the long hours of darkness she would seek out the attention of young John in his charcoal burner's crude hut. The result was that she was expecting his child and John, in June 1789, was obliged to forsake his real love and marry Jane.

Almost at once, married life became intolerable. She was a drunk and made his life a misery; nagging, taunting, teasing, humiliating him and reducing the previously lovable, mild-mannered John to a shrivelling wreck.

Matters came to a head on the night of 5th July 1789 when after a heavy drinking session at the nearby Castle of Comfort Inn, she pushed him too far. He walked out, leaving her to find her own way home. She followed and let loose with a barrage of venomous insults. Something inside him snapped. He took her by the throat and shook her uncontrollably, then wrenched a post from the hedge and beat her unconscious. Still out of control, he slit her throat.

He made a poor job of hiding her body, which was found a few days later when Jane's father organised a search party. It was discovered in the hollow of a prehistoric 'bank and ditch', henceforth called 'Dead Woman's Ditch' and labelled as such on Ordnance Survey maps. John admitted his guilt immediately and was taken off to Bridgwater to await his trial. Lord Kenyon presided and, because of John's confession, it was no more than a formality. The death sentence was announced, with his body to be given up for dissection. The public, however, voiced their objections. There had been far too many murders of late. They wanted his body to be left to rot on the gibbet. The judge conceded to their cries.

The following day John, shackled around the neck, wrists and ankles, made the cart-drawn journey to Nether Stowey. At the village, the preparations at the gibbet were not yet complete and John's torment was prolonged. Up on the hillside, the villagers were already gathering, but were somewhat more subdued than at most hangings. These were John's neighbours and friends. They knew that he was deep-down a decent fellow, popular and kind. Amongst them was his former true love, Ann Rice. When the cart arrived, the villagers as one turned their backs away from the centre stage. Ann walked forward, eyes focused only on John. The villagers and execution party afforded them their moment of privacy, final words of parting passing between them. As Ann attempted a kiss of forgiveness, she was held back and then lowered from the cart.

With the noose around John's neck, the cart pulled forward as the horse's rump received a hefty slap. John's remains were placed in a cage and left hanging from the gibbet for a full year, providing yet another lasting place name for the Ordnance Survey maps, 'Walford's Gibbet'.

Buried with a stake through her heart

John Walford's sister-in-law was perhaps another victim of the tragic story of John Walford. Sarah Walford also felt the shame and the loss of her husband's brother. When her own husband died, she could face life alone no longer and in 1821 committed suicide. It was not permissible for a suicide victim to be placed in consecrated ground and consequently she was buried

Bincombe Cross where Sarah Walford lies with a stake through her heart.

at Bincombe Cross, a crossroads just above her home village of Nether Stowey on the road to Dead Woman's Ditch. As was the practice in such times, she was interred after having a stake driven through her heart.

It is interesting to note that this happened at a time when a suicide attempt could be guaranteed to be successful, even if at first it wasn't. Until 1823 suicide was a capital offence. If you tried it and failed, you would be brought before the court for the crime of attempted suicide and if you were found guilty, the punishment was death. You couldn't go wrong!

Another such site is at Wiveliscombe at the junction of Tytibye Lane, a little road that runs uphill alongside Greenway Cottage in North Street, and Jews Lane, a bridleway. Tytibye Lane takes its name from the suicide victim who was buried there at the junction, again with a stake through his heart.

The county's final execution at the scene of the crime

The village of Kenn, near Nailsea, was the location for Somerset's final public execution at the scene of the crime. In 1830 William Wall ran an unlicensed cider house. A blind eye was normally turned towards such establishments but someone reported him to the authorities. Wall suspected it was a local farmhand working for his neighbour Benjamin Poole. Either as an act of revenge or intimidation prior to his court case, he persuaded 32-year-old

John Rowley and 19-year-old Richard Clarke to burn down three stacks of Poole's wheat valued at £50.

At the ensuing trial, all three were found guilty and condemned to death. This act of agricultural arson and intimidation was on the very doorsteps of the county's Chief Constable and High Sheriff, both of whom lived within a few miles of Kenn. Perhaps therein lies the reason why the execution was held at the scene of the crime.

On 8th September 1830, some 15,000 spectators arrived to witness the event. A hanging was considered to provide a good day's entertainment and perhaps many of those present were aware of the changing mood towards public executions and realised this might be their last chance to witness such a spectacle.

For the condemned men and the execution party, it was to be a long day, starting with their departure from Ilchester gaol at 4 o'clock in the morning on their 42-mile journey, the prisoners seated on their coffins as they travelled. At Axbridge they were met by the High Sheriff's javelin men. At Kenn they were joined by 150 of the Chief Constable's men. They arrived around midday to the sound of the funeral bell. The police officers formed a line along the route to ensure that there would be no interference from the expectant crowd as the execution party journeyed from the Drum and Monkey public house. Prison governor, chaplain, High Sheriff, magistrates and local councillors formed the official party. Bringing up the rear was an open top wagon in which the prisoners stood in clear view of the now somewhat hostile crowd who hurled torrents of abuse at the three men.

At the roughly assembled gallows, in the seven-acre field adjacent to that in which the stacks of corn had been burned, the local vicar read a number of prayers to the kneeling prisoners. Across the gallows was a notice declaring 'For firing ricks'. Black hoods were pulled over their heads. Their feet and hands were tied. Rowley pleaded with his family and friends to learn their lesson from his mistakes and Wall declared that he should have listened to his wife and never opened a cider house. Standing in the back of the cart on which they arrived, the nooses were placed around their necks, the horse's rump was slapped, the cart pulled forward and the three dropped to meet their maker. Rowley and Wall twitched momentarily as life extinguished. For poor Clarke, being younger and lighter, the executioner had misjudged the length of the drop required to effect a rapid death. He convulsed at the end of the rope until two of the execution party hung from his legs to hasten the end of his unnecessary suffering.

It was all over by lunchtime. The bodies were returned to Ilchester gaol for burial in an unmarked grave. Mary, the wife of William Wall, was one of four others involved who had been found guilty at the same trial but their punishment was deportation. For Mary this was preceded by thirteen months in prison where her eighth child was born.

The Bridgwater Borough Police Force in 1890, with its superintendent, two sergeants and nine constables.

Around and about the county

The majority of public executions took place at Ilchester, runner-up spot being Taunton's Wilton gaol, and then latterly at Shepton Mallet prison, albeit these were in private. However, there were a significant number of public executions right across the county:

Bath, Odd Down

1748	Richard Biggs	Murder	Hanged

Bedminster Down

1740	John Millard	Highway Robbery	Hanged in chains
1783	George Gaynes	Theft	Hanged

Black Down

1746	Francis Wilkins	Murder of Jane Wilkins	Hanged in chains

Bridgwater

1785	William Stiles	Murder of Richard Hole	Hanged at Hamp Green

| 1795 | William White | Murder of Maria Bailey | Hanged |
| 1801 | John Craigel | Murder of John Salway | Hanged |

Brislington Common

| 1740 | Cornelius York | Highway robbery | Hanged in chains |

Chilton Heath

| 1746 | Marey John Galway | Murder of Ann Pool | Hanged in chains |

Ilton

| 1799 | Richard Williams | Murder of Thomas Laver | Hanged Afterwards in chains |

Kenn, Nailsea

1830	William Wall	Arson	Hanged
	Richard Clarke	Arson	Hanged
	John Rowley	Arson	Hanged

Kingston St Mary

| | Samuel Yendall | Burglary | Hanged at Dodwell Green |

Nether Stowey

| 1789 | John Walford | Murder of his wife, Jane | Hanged at Doddington Green Afterwards in chains |

Taunton (outside the Wilton gaol or at the Stone Gallows)

1747	John Bailey	Murder of Thomas Knight	Hanged
1762	John Ham	Horse theft	Hanged
1770	Nehemiah Webber	Murder of William Gough	Hanged
1770	Stephen Scudder	Murder of William Gough	Hanged
1783	William Lattimore	Highway robbery	Hanged
1793	Joan Tattel	Murder of bastard child	Hanged
1789	John Isaacs	Murder of John Wilmot	Hanged
1801	Michael Day	Horse theft	Hanged
1801	Peter Kingdom	Cattle theft	Hanged
1801	George Tout	Sheep Theft	Hanged
1809	James Taylor	Murder	Hanged
1810	Thomas Gage	Murder of Sarah Stirling	Hanged

11

WILTON – THE COUNTY BRIDEWELL

By 1843 Ilchester gaol had fulfilled its role as the county gaol, and Wilton gaol, which was already in existence in Taunton, took on that county role, becoming known as the county bridewell, an archaic name for prison. Preceding that date, only relatively minor offenders were held at this gaol. One of the most amusing is the tale of Mary Hamilton, alias Charles or George Hamilton, dating back to 1746. Yes, she was a cross-dresser and was sentenced to be whipped for pretending to be a man and perhaps more seriously for marrying no fewer than fourteen wives! Henry Fielding recorded the event as:

The woman (yes, woman) who had fourteen wives

> ... *was try'd for pretending herself a man, and marrying 14 Wives ... After a debate of the nature of the crime, and what to call it, it was agreed that she was an uncommon, notorious cheat, and sentenc'd to be publickly whipt ... to be imprison'd for 6 months.*

The records for 1814 provide a range of other petty crimes: Catharine Carral stole banknotes; James Hawkins, alias House stole money; James Horsey – assault on a girl; John Lear stole a book at Taunton; Mary Millett, apprentice at Wiveliscombe, ran away; Mary Mullins of Broomfield stole clothes; Benjamin Philips of Taunton stole spoons and John Pym of Pitminster stole hay.

These were all minor offences but there were more serious cases. One example from 1812 was that of Thomas Venn, the son of an East Brent farmer. He had got Elizabeth Coomer pregnant and was desperate for her to blame anyone other than himself. He agreed to meet her at night in a field, prior to which he went to the local inn and bought a pint of brandy, borrowing a glass at the same time. He met Elizabeth near the bank of the river and that was the last anyone saw of her alive. Later investigation found their footprints at the edge of the river and her stomach contents held the full pint of brandy. The outcome of the trial is not known, which would suggest that he was found not guilty.

James Turle, keeper of Wilton gaol

James Turle, the one-time keeper of Wilton gaol, was born in Taunton in 1778. In 1802 he married Elizabeth Westcott and two years later they had a daughter. He was an innkeeper and was sufficiently comfortable in life to make a donation to Taunton Hospital in 1810. That same year, and perhaps because of his apparent generosity, he was also appointed to the position of sheriff's officer and in that role became keeper of Wilton gaol. Now the two occupations do seem to fit together rather nicely if we remember that prisoners had to pay for those little comforts in life such as a jug of ale, and it could only be done through the keeper of the prison. Perhaps he abused the privilege because in October 1813 he was dismissed from the position for misconduct. It was just nine months after his wife had died and perhaps therein lies part of the explanation. He continued life as an innkeeper, remarried the following year and twelve months further on he returned to his position as sheriff's officer and re-established the combined roles of inn and gaol keeper until his death in 1835.

During Turle's period of service, a committee report was produced in 1825 that described the gaol as having 60 to 70 prisoners, separated into eleven lime-washed departments with the turnkey's room in the centre. Prisoners were fed with a pint and a half of oatmeal gruel, twelve ounces of potatoes, six ounces of scrap beef and a pound of bread per day. The governor's house formed part of the exterior of the prison and from it a passage ran down through the middle of the custodial section. The report commented that Wilton gaol was to have a tread-wheel built for milling grain. There would eventually be two wheels, each capable of holding 30 prisoners at any one time. The female prisoners, in common with the practice in other gaols in the county, were mainly employed in laundry work. Unlike Ilchester, Wilton still kept selected prisoners in chains and was proud of its record of no escapes. On the day of assizes elsewhere around the county, Bridgwater or Wells for example, as many as 70 prisoners going to trial would be transported in covered wagons with locked doors and bars on the windows.

Taking over from Ilchester

Although Wilton gaol was not officially the county prison until 1843, the migration of prisoners from Ilchester to Wilton started much earlier, especially when it was time for the county assizes to be held. A newspaper report from the *Taunton Courier* describes the scene in November 1833:

> *Yesterday, several vans full of prisoners from Ilchester and Shepton Mallet gaols, arrived in this town, and deposited their miserable loads*

at Wilton gaol preparatory to the Assizes, which commence in town tomorrow, with the usual formalities. There are two hundred and five prisoners for trial, between eighty and ninety of whom are charged with capital offences.

Hard labour

A common punishment for the inmates at Wilton was hard labour, which was long hours of back-breaking stone-crushing with sledge-hammers, making the fine stone required for road maintenance. George Lilly in 1834 received five months' hard labour for assaulting a police constable. In 1851 James Norman, alias prisoner 403, was sentenced to 14 days' hard labour for malicious trespass, which was probably poaching.

Front door executions

When a crime was of a serious nature and the death penalty was imposed, the executions from Wilton gaol would normally take place outside the front door. The final such public execution took place in 1867 but before then there was a well-recorded event in the spring of 1861 at the execution of Matthew Wedmore.

Matthew was born in the north Somerset village of Failand in 1826. He was the eldest of twelve children in the family of Samuel, a rabbit dealer, and Sarah Wedmore. At the age of 18, Matthew joined the Royal Marines and after his discharge he was a labourer and waterman at the quayside in Bristol. Meanwhile Charles, one of his brothers, had also joined the army and was on home leave for the Christmas break in 1860. It turned out to be a week in which Charles spent most of his time drinking or sleeping it off. He became determined not to return to life in the army and decided that there were easier ways to make money.

The two brothers had an uncle, George Waterman, who lived with his wife in nearby Dundry, in a lonely cottage with a one-acre garden. They were elderly and enjoyed a simple life, spending little or no money and creating the impression that they had plenty but hoarded it. It was the prospect of 'hidden treasure' that drew Charles and Matthew Wedmore to George Waterman's abode. Charles had already visited Dundry a few days before in order to visit another brother, William, who had bought a house from the uncle. Not being familiar with the village, Charles sought guidance from John Keevil, a stable-hand at the vicarage, who had also once been the village policeman in nearby Winford. Keevil led Charles to his uncle's cottage where he knocked on the door and announced himself as 'the old policeman of Winford'. This gave confidence to the old man, who willingly opened the door.

When Charles and Matthew revisited the house with the intent to rob, Charles impersonated Keevil and announced himself to be 'the old policeman of Winford'. The door was opened and in they went, complete with two big sticks cut from the hedgerow to be used as clubs. Inside, the elderly lady sat sewing by the fire hearth, and watched in horror as they battered her husband and demanded that he hand over all his money. They ransacked the house and took silver coins, two silver watches, a bottle of brandy, a silk handkerchief and two loaded pistols, which the old man kept beneath his pillow. Matthew dragged George to an outhouse at the back of the cottage and there tied him up. His brother Charles joined him, declaring that he had put the old lady to sleep. The badly beaten George was then told not to move until his wife woke up to release him. The two brothers, having filled what little space they had left in their pockets with bacon and bread, made their getaway.

George's wife never recovered but just lay there unconscious. George, however, managed to work free from his bonds and headed up the road to a neighbour, who called for the police. The search for the two brothers was on and it became a murder hunt when the old lady died later that evening.

The brothers were spotted by an observant landlord when they tried to pawn one of the stolen watches. The police were discreetly notified and arrived to arrest them. Charles attempted to shoot one of the officers but fortunately missed, despite his military training. All the evidence required was found on them, including the best part of the stolen items. At the inquest at the Dundry Inn, death was announced as caused by compression of the brain from a fracture of the skull, the result of four blows to the head. George was too badly injured to attend his wife's funeral, having himself received six blows to the head. He eventually moved in with his nephew William, who lived nearby.

Brought to trial, the two brothers began to blame each other and, in so doing, only helped to confirm all the evidence given by George Waterman. The jury found them guilty of murder and they were sentenced to death, to be hanged outside the door of Wilton gaol, opposite Taunton's Shire Hall. As they left the gaol for the last time, the procession was headed by the chaplain reading the burial service, followed by the governor of the gaol and then the brothers. The local paper described the scene:

The sun shone brightly this morning upon the crowd assembled in front of Taunton Gaol, to witness the execution of the Brothers Wedmore, for the terrible murder at Dundry, of Mrs. Waterman. It is calculated that as many as seven thousand persons were present.

At least their final day was blessed with good weather.

Taunton Police Station, formerly Wilton gaol, proudly displays its traditional blue lights.

12

TRANSPORTATION

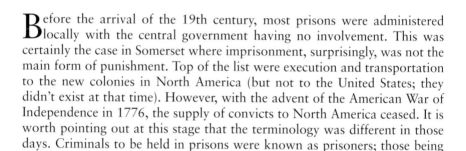

Before the arrival of the 19th century, most prisons were administered locally with the central government having no involvement. This was certainly the case in Somerset where imprisonment, surprisingly, was not the main form of punishment. Top of the list were execution and transportation to the new colonies in North America (but not to the United States; they didn't exist at that time). However, with the advent of the American War of Independence in 1776, the supply of convicts to North America ceased. It is worth pointing out at this stage that the terminology was different in those days. Criminals to be held in prisons were known as prisoners; those being transported, even if temporarily held in prisons, were known as convicts.

With the American outlet drying up, the prisons soon began to overflow and disused ships were brought into service as prison ships, or hulks as they were known. On arrival, the prisoners were stripped and washed, then issued with coarse jackets and trousers and placed in leg irons. Their daily diet was 20 ounces of bread and a quart of gruel. Four days a week they were given meat weighing 14 ounces before being cooked. During the day, they would work on shore, heavy labouring work.

This was how the convicts were held until there were sufficient to fill a ship for transportation to Australia, initially to New South Wales, to the infamous Botany Bay, and after 1830 to Van Diemen's Land, or Tasmania as it was later to be named. In the case of Somerset's convicts, initially held in Ilchester gaol, they were mostly transferred to hulks in Plymouth, but also to Woolwich and other sites, depending on available capacity. In the years from 1787 when the transportation began to Australia, through to 1867 when it came to an end, over 160,000 convicts were transported in this way.

Life on board

Life on board the prison ships was hard, even severe. The convicts were housed below decks on the 'prison deck'. This was well down in the ship, with little or no natural light. Those prisoners considered to be higher risk were also in cells behind bars, and the highest risk inmates even in chains. Occasional visits were allowed to the main deck for fresh air and exercise.

The early voyages, perhaps because they were being scrutinised, were fairly successful, with few or no deaths during the journey. But on later trips, especially where the responsibility was franchised out, the captains and crew could be cruel masters, with little compassion for the convicts. Poor diet and conditions resulted in a dramatic increase in the 'en voyage' death toll. From 1801 the number of sailings was reduced to just two a year, taking advantage of the improved southern hemisphere weather. These set off in May and September, hence convicts could wait for several months in the hulks before their departure. Conditions also improved when the captains were given a bonus system based on the number of safe arrivals. Ships by 1840 were also taking 'chaplains' to see to both spiritual needs and the education of the transportees.

On arrival in Australia, the individuals would typically be allocated to property owners, farmers or merchants and would be watched over by regular troops. Skilled workers, masons and carpenters were much in demand and could fare well if they kept their noses clean. Those with literacy skills could likewise find appropriate work but the majority were agricultural labouring material and life for them could be particularly hard, depending on to whom they were allocated. For many, Botany Bay was their first sight of the new land but the area had a problem – the lack of fresh water – and so there was a general migration north to Parramatta, which has since developed eastwards to become the enormous city of Sydney.

Although many were deported for life, they could still gain their freedom, which came on completing the allotted sentence period but could be achieved quicker with good behaviour. Pardons could be granted and were either conditional, in which case no return to Britain was permitted, or absolute when the convict was free to return. Most, but not all, of them stayed. The problem was that the majority couldn't afford the fare home, and others preferred not to return with the stigma of being an ex-convict. And so in their thousands they stayed, married and raised a new nation.

Mary Ford

Little is known of Mary Ford other than that she was a Somerset woman who was tried at the Taunton Assizes in 1797, found guilty of theft and sentenced to transportation. Her story is of interest partly because she was the first Somerset transportee I have uncovered from this period, and secondly because of the success she made once resident in Australia.

Richard Fitzgerald was another transportee sentenced to seven years. He came from a wealthy and well-connected family and aged just 15, in 1787, was found guilty of an unknown crime at the Westminster Quarter Sessions. He spent the next four years awaiting transportation, finally arriving in Australia in 1791. Perhaps his family connections can explain the lack of records as to the nature of his crime. It certainly explains the most unusual circumstances whereby he arrived as a convict bringing with him what were described as considerable 'private assets', and once in Australia, he was described as showing remarkable activity and regular conduct. With a great depth of agricultural experience, a succession of governors gave him responsibility for running a number of farms and in 1792, by which time his seven years had been served, he was given the post of superintendent of convicts at Toongabbie, his area of responsibility being extended the following year to include Parramatta. In 1802 he was inspector and governor of all the farming ventures belonging to the Crown. He also held over 300 acres in his own name.

It was at this time that he met Somerset's Mary Ford, no doubt in his role as convict supervisor or inspector. The couple were to live together and the relationship produced three sons, albeit outside of marriage. We know that Mary was a married woman when she was transported and can only assume that her husband lived on but eventually died, for in June 1815 Mary and Richard Fitzgerald were finally married. When Fitzgerald died in 1840, his estate was valued at £34,000 and he had even been one of the early proprietors of the Bank of New South Wales. He had been a Freemason and had considerably influenced the birth and shaping of the city of Sydney.

Mary Ford must have despaired on her trial day at the Taunton Assizes but her story just goes to show how, as one door closes, another opens.

Joseph Carter of East Brent and Matthew Pittman of Westonzoyland

On a September night in 1814, Joseph Carter, a labourer from East Brent, broke into the house of Richard Colson and took away nine handkerchiefs valued at four shillings each, twenty yards of cotton worth twenty shillings (£1), sixteen yards of linen cloth to the value of forty shillings (£2), sixty yards of ribbon worth thirty shillings and six yards of corduroy also worth thirty shillings, altogether totalling over £7. At his trial at the Somerset Assizes, he was found guilty and having no means of paying recompense was condemned to be hanged. As was common, on appeal this was reduced to transportation for life, the sentence reflecting the high value of the goods stolen.

Life began again for Joseph once in Australia. He married another transportee and they had a daughter Anne, who in turn married another transportee, William Smith. Having produced three sons, William died and Anne remarried, this time to James Pittman, the son of John Matthew Pittman, another convict from Westonzoyland in her father's home county of Somerset. Having been found guilty at the Bridgwater Assizes in 1814 for stealing a horse from Crewkerne, he was transported the following year. These stories illustrate how new lives could blossom for adults sentenced to transportation, but not all those sailing were adult, many were very young children.

Children of the hulks

Grand larceny sounds so serious. Stealing the Crown jewels, a gold bullion robbery, defrauding a bank of millions all come to mind but in the 19th century grand larceny was simply the theft of any item over a given value, perhaps £1. By today's standards, a youngster shoplifting an iPod would be guilty of grand larceny and historically would have been condemned to death or, more likely, transportation. That was the fate that befell 12-year-old James Carter, 15-year-old Charles Old and 16-year-old Charles Haines, all Somerset lads who were found guilty at the October 1823 assizes held at Taunton. Their punishment was a sentence of seven years' transportation to Australia.

That same year, a ship by the name of the *Bellerophon* was moored up at Sheerness. She had once been a proud 74-gun man-of-war and could boast of having been the ship that brought Napoleon to England after the Battle of Waterloo. Approaching her final retirement, she had been converted to use as a prison ship. Below decks, where guns had once lined the portals, the lower decks now housed a series of iron-barred cells down either side, with a wide passageway along the centre. It was to this ship and these conditions that the three Somerset boys were delivered. John Steadman, in charge of the hulk, showed no mercy in his handling of young lads, the small weaker ones being mixed with the larger bullies. It was down to them to sort out any problems. Perhaps Charles Haines, as the eldest of the Somerset trio, was one of those less well-behaved bullies, for two years later he is recorded as on board the *Medway*, on his way to Van Diemen's Land, where there was a far harsher and stricter regime.

Henry Savery, Australia's first novelist

Henry Savery gave every impression of a man doomed to failure. Born in Somerset in 1791, he had a privileged upbringing as the son of a Bristol banker and had the benefit of a grammar school education. He was to marry Eliza Elliott Oliver, the daughter of a London businessman, and their only son, Henry Oliver, was born in 1816. Henry senior proved to be a poor businessman. An attempt to run a sugar refinery ended in bankruptcy in 1819. For the next two years he unsuccessfully tried his hand at producing the *Bristol Observer* before returning to sugar refining and further disasters. Having allowed the business to lapse into debt, he tried to find his way out by forging bills of credit to the enormous tune of £30,000. He did a quick moonlight flit, leaving his partner in the lurch. His partner set off in hot pursuit and found Savery aboard the *Hudson*, a ship moored up at Cowes and which half an hour later would have been bound for America.

In April 1825 Savery pleaded guilty to his crimes and was sentenced to be hanged three weeks later. The day before his planned execution, his appeal for clemency finally succeeded and his sentence was reduced to transportation to Van Diemen's Land. In August of that year, as one of over 170 convicts, he sailed aboard the *Medway* bound for Hobart harbour.

He appeared to land on his feet, being given employment initially in the service of the Colonial Secretary's office and then with the Colonial Treasurer, an amazing achievement for someone so dishonest with money and apparently not that bright at handling figures. However, he was able to persuade his wife that his position was so good that she should sail for Australia and join him. That she did and was ably chaperoned by the colony's Attorney General, who perhaps looked after her too well and indeed it appears that a relationship had developed between the pair, which was to create problems later for Henry Savery.

By the time Eliza arrived, Henry's position had foundered. He was once again experiencing financial problems and was imprisoned for debt. Within three months Eliza had left with their son, never to see her husband again. It was downhill for Henry after that. He even tried to commit suicide by slashing his throat, only to be saved by the prison doctor.

Henry used his time in prison to write about life as a convict and life in Van Diemen's Land. His sketches were published in the *Colonial Times* under the pseudonym of Simon Stukeley. In time there were sufficient sketches to make a book, which was published as *The Hermit of Van Diemen's Land*. Whilst not a classic piece of writing, it nonetheless created great interest and became a best seller. His use of a pseudonym was essential for, at the time, it was a crime for convicts to publish and his first novel was no doubt written secretly whilst in prison. It was to be entitled *Quintus Servinton: A Tale founded upon Incidents of Real Occurrences* and was published anonymously in 1831. It was Australia's first novel and its actual author was probably Australia's worst kept secret. It was largely biographical and served then as a plea for a change to the cruel conditions that prevailed and today as a window into Australia's past.

The following year, Henry was granted his ticket of leave, only to be re-arrested for having published articles in a provincial journal. He was soon released and rented a farm. Sadly, debts and alcoholism were to be his ruin and by 1840 he was back to his forgery tricks and up before the magistrate, who just happened to be the very same man with whom his wife had the affair! He was sentenced to imprisonment in Port Arthur, known for its harsh conditions and high death rate. It was there that this son of Somerset died. He was buried on the Isle of the Dead, just off the coast, where prisoners and staff were given their last resting place.

The Hockeys of Shepton Mallet

Oh what a family! Daniel Hockey and his wife, Ann Reakes, produced at least three sons and three daughters. Jane came first, born in Ditcheat in 1802, followed by James in Evercreech in 1806, and then Samuel (1811), Eliza (1812), Charlotte (1818) and Charles (1820) who were all born in Shepton Mallet, where the family had finally settled.

Samuel was the first to be tried for criminal activities when, as a 12-year-old, he was convicted to one month in prison for stealing a pound of suet, but six years later, in 1829, the stolen item was a little larger and a little more serious. In June of that year he had stolen a donkey valued at £1 from Edward Kent of

Shepton Mallet. Now how you hide a stolen donkey is beyond me. They are not the quietest of animals and it makes me wonder if the theft was perhaps the result of some dispute rather than a 'theft by stealth' situation. However, since he was following in his father's footsteps as a butcher, perhaps his purpose was to quietly and quickly dispose of the beast. This is borne out by the fact that just two days earlier than the theft of Edward Kent's donkey, he had also stolen one belonging to John Forward at Pilton. Whatever the cause or reason, on 1st August 18-year-old Samuel appeared at the Bridgwater Assizes accused of the theft. At his trial he was described as being 5 foot 4 inches tall, grey-eyed, fair and slender, with the ability to read but not write.

When the trial ended three weeks later on 22 August, he was found guilty and sentenced to 14 years' transportation. Incredible as it may seem, his older brother James, now aged 23, was also up before the very same assizes. James was already married to Rachael Bafue and was living at Ashwick with their two children, near to the family home. He and a friend Cornelius Loxton had been charged with the theft on 4th May of that year of a saddle valued at £1, and a bridle worth 5 shillings, the property of William Hyatt of Shepton Mallet. However, they were also charged with the theft just nine days later of a gelding valued at £20, the property of Henry Hodges of Doulting. This was a far more serious offence and it was for that crime that they were found guilty. Having spent May to August in Shepton Mallet prison, they were taken to the Bridgwater Assizes where, despite their pleas of innocence, they were condemned to be hanged, the sentence later commuted to transportation. And they were lucky, because these were not their first offences, both of them having been found guilty of felony, being a crime that involves the confiscation of the convicted person's land and goods, just two years earlier at the Taunton Assizes. All in all, it had been a bad day in court for the Hockey family.

Five days later, all three were transferred to Ilchester gaol prior to their transfer at the end of September to the prison hulk waiting at Plymouth, the aptly named *Captivity*, finally arriving in Van Diemen's Land aboard the *Sir Charles Forbes* in July 1830.

Samuel's conduct in Australia has been well documented, as it tends to be for trouble-makers. Repeated insolence, disobedience, threatening language, possessing a piece of pork for which he couldn't account and general misconduct were all included in his list of misdemeanours. His punishment list is as long as it was painful: 12 lashes on the breach; 25 lashes; 50 lashes; 10 days solitary; 3 days solitary; 3 months hard labour; 1 month hard labour; 12 months hard labour in chains. His behaviour as a convict fell well short of perfect but nonetheless by 1839 he had gained his ticket of leave.

In July 1838 he applied for permission to marry Tasmanian-born Ellen Barefoot and permission was duly granted. But perhaps Ellen was aware of his character for she never took up the offer and instead married an Edward Cassidy in the February of the following year. Samuel's heart appears not to have been too damaged for later that same year, in December 1839, he married Ellen's sister, Bridget Barefoot. His brother James also was to marry one of the Barefoot sisters, this time Ann, and the brothers reunited to travel, both by sea and land, with their young families to reach Victoria. The journey could not have been easy as it is recorded that they were to bury a child at the foot of Blue Mountain near Blackwood on the way.

Samuel had at least two daughters who survived, Isabella born around 1840, and Ann, born December 1842. She was christened on the same day as Eliza, the daughter of James and Ann. By the mid-1850s Samuel had spent some time in the goldfields and had established himself as the owner of a brickyard and shopkeeper with a store in Victoria Street in Geelong. Perhaps it was his money that was to pay for his now elderly parents to join him in August 1854, along with his widowed sister Charlotte and her four daughters. It was the first time the parents had seen their son in 24 years, and for Charlotte the first time since she was 10 years old.

Meanwhile, Cornelius Loxton had also carved out a new life for himself. Having married Julia Butler, they raised seven offspring. He died in Australia aged 64.

Isaac Parkhouse of Twerton, Bath

Isaac Parkhouse was born around 1813, the son of Daniel and Mary Parkhouse of Twerton, Bath. Aged 19 he was living in St James Place in Bath but it was in the north Somerset village of Wrington that in 1832 he and an associate named H. Bartlett assaulted Isaac Gladstone and Joseph Hill. Little is known of the circumstances but we are told that the two were brought to trial in April of that year, found guilty and sentenced to death. As anticipated, their sentences were reduced to transportation for life. In April 1833, after over a year on a prison hulk, the pair of them set sail from Plymouth aboard the *Atlas*, bound for Australia. One hundred and sixteen days later they arrived at Hobart.

Parkhouse was known as prisoner P951, the P being the first letter of his name and the 951 indicating that there had been 950 convicts before him with surnames beginning with P. It looks as though Parkhouse had kept a relatively clean sheet on his way over since we find him allocated to a Mr John Knight, whom he remained with for at least four years. The only blemish on his convict record was that he was found in an ale house, for which he was sentenced to six hours in the stocks.

In 1841 he was granted his ticket of leave and a good conduct document, which meant he could then seek paid employment. In 1848, aged 35, he married Mary Smith, a fellow convict, and settled down to a trade – first as a carter and later as a horse dealer and livery stable keeper. The couple had no children of their own but adopted Ellen Mary, who would later marry a butcher. His wife died aged 66 and Isaac died some years later, aged 85. In his will he had left what proved to be a considerable estate to be shared between the three brothers he had left behind in Bath.

Elizabeth Cross of Rimpton

Having a previous conviction for theft, Elizabeth Cross was lucky to be working as a servant, but perhaps her employer was unaware of her misdemeanor. She worked for John Lockyer who lived at Rimpton and it was from his house that she stole a gold ring and a mixture of bedding and clothing in July 1842. The following month she was tried at the county assizes and sentenced to transportation for seven years. Not two years had passed when she sought approval as a convict to marry. Permission was granted and she married John Whitbourne, a free settler, in Hobart. Life was starting to improve.

They had two children before they left Tasmania to settle in Victoria in 1847 where a further ten children were born. Elizabeth's husband died in the early part of 1873 and within two years she had remarried. She died in Collingwood, Victoria in 1896, a free woman with a considerable legacy by way of the children she had left behind.

William Langdon, horse thief

William Langdon was brought before the Somerset Assizes in the early part of 1839, accused of stealing two mares the previous December. Short in height and sallow in complexion, the 45-year-old blacksmith faced the bench as his wife and seven children heard the verdict. Guilty – sentenced to 15 years transportation to Van Diemen's Land. He was transferred to a prison hulk at Gosford and arrived in Hobart in the January of 1840. There he was given a succession of jobs with various employers and was considered a reliable and worthy man.

In 1842 Mary, who was his second wife, followed him to the colonies with their children and their granddaughter Elizabeth. William was eventually sent to the Police Magistrate at Hamilton where he was granted his ticket of leave. He settled in Hamilton and lived as a farmer, on a property owned by his son William junior, until his death in August 1873. Mary died the following year, aged 90, and was buried with William.

*   *   *

The above were just a few of the hundreds of Somerset folk transported to Australia. Those with the willingness to learn from their mistakes, and showing the resourcefulness to work hard and stay honest, survived to become the founders of a formidable nation.

13

SHEPTON MALLET – COUNTY HOUSE OF CORRECTION

Hard labour

We all know what a hamster looks like as it merrily gallops away inside an exercise wheel. It's amusing to watch and presumably the hamster enjoys the experience since it keeps going back for more. Now imagine a tread-wheel – built in the same fashion, but large enough to take a man. Then expand the wheel so that it can simultaneously take several men, who will be forced to rotate the wheel for hours at a time to the point where the commonest injury is a hernia. Shepton Mallet prison contained no fewer than six tread-wheels of different sizes, presumably according to the size of the prisoners and the number available. That was just one of the scenes inside the prison from 1823, when the first wheel was constructed. There would eventually be another five tread-wheels in total, each driving its own mill, until they were removed in 1890.

The wheels were used to power a grain mill, which was located just outside the prison wall, so those grinding the grain would perhaps be unaware of the suffering within. The tread-wheel was just one of the forms of hard labour within the prison where, in common with the workhouses, another task was that of breaking stones to create the materials for maintaining the road surfaces around the north of Somerset. The tread-wheel, however, presented an opportunity in 1860 for at least one prisoner, ironically named Judge, which he was quick to seize. The shaft that connected the tread-wheel to the mill passed through a 2-ft-wide tunnel in the thick prison wall, a gap that proved large enough to permit his escape, albeit he was later recaptured in Shaftesbury.

It is easy to understand how desperate the prisoners were to escape when the conditions of those times are revealed. The prison opened in the early 17th century as a 'house of correction' and as such can claim to be the oldest occupied prison still on its original site. Conditions were tough within its walls. Men, women and children were all held together, in the 'care' of unpaid gaolers whose only source of income was from fees paid by the prisoners themselves or by their friends or family. The payment of such fees ensured sufficient food or perhaps the luxury of liquor in some cases. A commissioner's report to Parliament in 1773 described how prisoners entered in a healthy condition but were reduced to emaciated objects within just a few months, many dying from malnutrition, fever or diseases such as smallpox.

It was no wonder that escapes were attempted, but generally unsuccessful. Prisoner Jeffreys, a sheep stealer, escaped in 1765 only to be recaptured ten days later in Lyme Regis, perhaps hoping to flee the country. Mary Harris escaped in 1776 and as far as I know was never recaptured. The bounty on her head rose to 20 guineas by the following year. James Thompson (1819), Daniel James (1866) and Samuel Glover Fudge (1878) were also escapees who were all recaptured, typically after a few months, and the penalty for escaping was generally further weeks of hard labour added to the end of their sentence.

By 1790 conditions had improved marginally with the addition of extra buildings, allowing men and women to be housed separately. A few years later it was being used for French prisoners during the Napoleonic War.

In a report of 1823, produced by the committee of the Society for Improvement of Prisons, Shepton Mallet gaol held about 200 prisoners with a turnover of seven to eight hundred per year, roughly ten per cent being women. It described how the interior grounds of the prison were split into six sectors with a watch-tower placed centrally from which all areas could be viewed, including at night. On the roof of the mill house there was a wind vane, which had been crafted to feature a prisoner in the tread-wheel, with the wheel turning in the wind. A further report in 1842 described how there were as many as eight prisoners to a cell and prisoners sleeping on the floor through lack of beds. Despite this apparent overcrowding, the following year Ilchester gaol was closed with its 'guests' being transferred to Shepton Mallet. The number of inmates peaked at around 270 and by 1897 had declined to just 61.

Executions

Until 1889, Ilchester and then Taunton had been the places for executions. Then the responsibility was handed over to Shepton Mallet and remained there until 1926. Samuel Rylands was the first for the drop, guilty of the murder of a young girl. Two years later, Henry Dainton suffered the same fate for the murder in Bath of his wife Hannah. Two years later and we find the records of Charles Squires, executed for the murder of a child.

We then come to November 1914 and the first hanging that we can find under the control of the famous Thomas Pierrepoint. This was the execution of Henry Pugsley who shot dead his neighbour, bringing an end to a long-standing and bitter feud. His story is retold in *Somerset Tales of Mystery and Murder*. Three more executions were to follow: the Australian soldier Verney Hasser in 1918, who had shot a fellow soldier and was hanged by John Ellis;

William Bignall, hanged by Robert Baxter, guilty of the murder of his girlfriend; and in 1926 what was to be the last civilian execution in Shepton gaol when Thomas Pierrepoint hanged John Lincoln, guilty of a murder in Trowbridge.

According to the tradition for such occasions, they were all buried in unmarked graves within the confines of the prison.

C block fire

In June 1904, on a warm Saturday evening that was about to get even hotter, the alarm was raised when it was realised that there was a fire in C block, almost certainly started by one of the prisoners. Within ten minutes the inmates had all been evacuated to the prison chapel and the town fire brigade, sponsored believe it or not by the local Anglo-Bavarian Brewery, were attacking the flames. Their sole efforts were never going to be enough to get the fire under control and by midnight the firemen from Wells had arrived, to be joined three hours later by their neighbours from Glastonbury and Frome. But they were not alone for not only did the warders join in, but also the prisoners themselves, working the manually operated fire pumps and manning the hoses on a rota basis.

When the fire finally came under control, a quick check of the inmates established that no one had escaped during the commotion and no one had been injured. Although the damage was extensive, the main fabric of the building, being stout grey stone, was as solid as ever and normal service was soon resumed.

By 1930 the number of prisoners had dwindled to around 50 and the decision was made to transfer the inmates and staff to prisons elsewhere, leaving the building to lie idle until the outbreak of war in 1939.

The Second World War – the Domesday Book and the GIs

The Second World War heralded a reopening of the prison at Shepton Mallet in October 1939. Firstly the prison was used to house a number of the nation's most historically important documents. With London suffering from heavy bombing, many of the country's treasures were at risk and the Domesday Book, a copy of the Magna Carta, dispatches from the Battle of Waterloo, the 'Peace in our time' declaration signed by Hitler, which Prime Minister Chamberlain negotiated, and the logbooks from Nelson's HMS *Victory* were transferred to the prison for safe keeping. Over 300 tons in total and far too much to have under one roof in times of conflict, especially with nearby Bristol and Bath as enemy bombing targets. Hence most of it was moved to other safe places, with the Domesday Book remaining for the duration of the conflict.

The other change was to reopen the prison to house military prisoners, initially for UK forces and then in 1942 it was handed over to the American

The execution block at Shepton Mallet prison.

authorities for use as their UK military prison. In accordance with the Visiting Forces Act of 1942, the Americans were allowed to dispense justice under the laws of their country rather than under British law. Hence it was here that, between 1942 and 1945, American soldiers found guilty of various crimes were executed, mostly by hanging but some by firing squad. Under British law, hanging was only used in cases of murder or high treason. Under American law, the death penalty also applied in cases of rape. Eighteen such executions took place in the single-windowed, two-storey building intrusively appended to one of the prison wings near the rear of the prison. Built of red brick, it was an eyesore, as ugly in its appearance as it was in its purpose, attached to a building now listed as Grade II for its historical and architectural significance.

On the inside of the main building, condemned cells were constructed and in the execution block the British-style gallows were installed. Of the eighteen executions, nine were for murder, six for rape and three for both. Two of those condemned were corporals and the rest privates. Privates David Cobb and Harold Smith were both sentenced to death by hanging for murdering fellow soldiers. Their executions were carried out by the famous and very professional Tom Pierrepoint. However, Private Alec Miranda, who murdered a sergeant whilst the sergeant was sleeping, was executed by firing squad, perhaps because there was a greater dishonour to death from a firing squad of your own troops. The background to this ignominious end was in Devon where Miranda, based at the Broomhill Camp, had gone out drinking, became drunk to the extent that he was taken by the military police back to the camp, and there, in a pique of anger, shot the sleeping Sergeant Thomas Evison. The other firing squad victim was Private Benjamin Pyke who, after kicking a fellow soldier in the groin, repeatedly stabbed him to death.

In both of these cases, the firing squad party was made up of eight soldiers. Each soldier was issued with a single shot to load, one of the eight being a blank, affording each of those involved the opportunity to believe that the execution was perhaps not his responsibility. The convicted man was led out to a yard where he was tied to a post, with a black hood being placed over his head. A ten-centimetre-wide white disc was then placed over the target area, the heart. The officer in charge then gave the commands to take positions, unlock rifles, aim and then fire. Should the firing squad have failed to kill the convicted man, then a sergeant was at hand to complete the execution. With one foot on the victim's head, he would fire a pistol shot into the head just behind the ear.

Corporal Ernest Lee Clarke and Privates Lee Davis and Augustine M. Guerra were all convicted of both rape and murder. Davis was executed by Albert Pierrepoint and his uncle Tom, the uncle and nephew now working in a partnership. Clarke and Guerra, who were responsible for the rape and death of a 15-year-old girl, were hanged side-by-side. Also hanged side-by-side were Corporal Robert L. Pearson and Private Parson Jones, guilty of the rape of a heavily pregnant woman.

Albert Pierrepoint also presided at the executions of Eliga Brinson, Willie Smith and Madison Thomas, all guilty of rape, whilst Tom Pierrepoint presided over the despatch of Wiley Harris, J.C. Leatherby and John H. Waters, all guilty of murder. Completing the list were Aniceto Martinez (rape of a 75-year-old woman and the last person to be hanged in Britain for this crime), William Harrison and George F. Smith (both for murder). Smith was actually executed on VE Day in 1945. All of these ceremonies were carried out under the control of either Albert or Thomas Pierrepoint, often assisting each other. At double executions, at least two other assistants were required. These included Herbert Morris, Alexander Riley and Steve Wade.

The Pierrepoints were the ultimate professionals when it came to hangings. Whilst the Americans used a standard length of rope with a coiled noose, all the Pierrepoint executions followed the British method with the length of rope determined according to the weight of the prisoner and with a noose in the British style. For their final few days before execution, the prisoners would be housed in the condemned cell and given the services of a prison chaplain. At the moment of execution of these American prisoners, the length of time it took before no heartbeat could be detected varied from three to twenty-two minutes. Whilst this may seem a painfully long time, what Albert Pierrepoint disliked intensely was the American practice of reading the death warrant to the prisoner at the gallows. This unnecessarily added several minutes to the agonising moments prior to despatch.

Post-war use

After VE Day the prison was returned to the British Army and used for soldiers who were close to their release dates. As an establishment it was famous for its extreme discipline and it needed to be with some of the characters who stayed there. Amongst those soldiers were the famous Kray twins and it was here that they met Charlie Richardson. Later they would take part in an East End gangland turf war during which Richardson became feared for his violent reprisal methods such as nailing his victims to the floor with 6-inch nails and then removing their toes with bolt-cutters. Men capable of those brutalities, it could be argued, needed a tough prison regime – or was it the regime that turned them into such thugs?

By 1966 the prison was entirely used for civilian purposes, mainly for those prisoners who would not be safe in other prisons, child molesters for example, and also for those prisoners who were considered to be sufficiently well behaved not to offer a threat. The following year the gallows were removed, allowing the one-time execution room to be converted to a library. In 1973 the prison's role was to change once more, this time to become a prison training centre, hopefully to provide its inmates with the skills to allow them to follow a normal life outside. This inevitably involved work experience outside the prison, providing plenty of opportunity for a quick getaway! At least eleven escaped this way but in all cases they were soon recaptured, most of them being found in one of the nearby pubs. Whilst those captured were usually punished by the addition of several weeks to the length of their sentence, one group on an outside party actually managed to get their sentence reduced. They were taking part in a gardening party when the elderly lady of the house collapsed inside. Using their experience from their days of crime, they broke into her house and helped to save the lady's life.

Other methods of escape included crawling through a barred toilet window and onto the roof; sawing the lock off a cell door; setting fire to bedding and then feigning unconsciousness to be taken to hospital; sawing through the bars of a window and climbing out using a rope of knotted bed sheets and even stealing a prison officer's car!

Today the prison is used for category 'C' life prisoners who are nearing the end of their term. At the time of writing the inmates number around 185, many of them having to share cells. These are predominantly murderers and sexual offenders with ages ranging up to 78 years old.

14

PRESENT-DAY REMINDERS

———————— ✳ ————————

Sites reminding us of crime and punishment are plentiful in the county, either in the form of place names or the buildings used as prisons or lock-ups, the latter being common in the villages and mainly used to hold drunks or trouble-makers. In most cases the offenders were released the following day, unless they were held pending collection by the constabulary to be taken elsewhere for trial. The usual structure of these lock-ups is a simple building, small in size with a single door and narrow window, but always built robustly from large stones or brick. Generally they are round or polygonal in shape. They proved useful throughout the centuries until the County Police Act of 1839 made them obsolete; consequently only a small number of them survive and they have been safeguarded by being given listed building status. With the advent of The Second World War, they also provided useful sentry boxes for the Home Guard and the occasional storage of arms.

Lock-ups

Castle Cary provides Somerset's best example of a surviving lock-up. It was built in circular fashion in 1799 and was constructed of stone with a domed roof. Its shape has provided it with the nickname of the 'pepper pot'. Although mainly used for drunks, it was also a place where children over seven years old who were found wandering the streets on a Sunday and not observing the Sabbath were held.

Kingsbury Episcopi's lock-up is octagonal with a stone roof boasting a ball finial. Built from

Castle Cary lock-up.

the local fawn-coloured Ham stone, it is placed centrally on the village green, its door quite narrow and the only other openings being two very narrow barred windows.

Meanwhile Monkton Combe, just a few miles south of Bath, can boast the 'Olde Lock Up', which was built around 1776 and differentiates itself from the others by being windowless. At Watchet the Court Leet lock-up can be found at the end of the town museum. It consists of a single cell tucked like a cupboard beneath the double-ended staircase leading to the chapel above.

Place-names

Evidence of past misdemeanours also survives in the use of place-names. In Bridgwater there is a road called **The Clink**. Whilst there is no firm evidence for the origin of this name, it has always been understood that 'clink' was a reference to an old lock-up. There is also a Clink and Clink Road in Frome. There are **Bridewell Lanes** in Loxton, Shapwick and Bath, 'bridewell' being an old name for a prison.

On the Quantock Hills, there are two well-known spots marked on the Ordnance Survey map as **Dead Woman's Ditch** and **Walford's Gibbet**, which relate to the murder of Jane Shorney by her husband John Walford (see Chapter 10). The ditch is the spot where he tried to hide her body, and the

Watchet's Court Leet lock-up can be seen at the Market House Museum.

gibbet is where he was hanged at the scene of his crime and then left to dangle in a cage for over a year, in clear view of his mother's front door.

Another gibbet reference comes with **Jack White's Gibbet** at a crossroads near Bratton Seymour (see again Chapter 10) and also in **Gibbet Road**, which leads to the crossroads from the south. The gibbet theme continues in Frome with **Gibbet Hill** to the west of the town.

Taunton has **Stonegallows,** a road just outside the town, another place of executions. Ilchester has its **Gallows Field**, also just outside the town. **Gallox Hill** and the **Gallox Bridge** (an historic monument and clapper bridge) at Dunster are both corruptions from the word 'gallows'. At Emborough at the Court Hotel will be found the **Hanging Tree**, a massive oak tree claimed to have been used for executions at the time of the Monmouth Rebellion.

Not as reminiscent of scenes of death, the **Pillory Cottage** at Old Cleeve provides a less gruesome place name and a lighter note on which to end our exploration of Somerset's crimes and punishments.

The Stone Gallows pub at Taunton marks the ancient location for executions.

Index